If I [Was] You

. . .

AND (ALOT) MORE GRAMMAR MISTAKES YOU MIGHT BE MAKING

LAUREN SUSSMAN

adamsmedia

Avon, Massachusetts

Published by
Adams Media, a division of F+W Media, Inc.
57 Littlefield Street, Avon, MA 02322. U.S.A.
www.adamsmedia.com

Contains material adapted and abridged from *The Everything® Grammar and Style Book, 2nd
Edition*, by Susan Thurman, copyright © 2008 by F+W Media, Inc., ISBN 10: 1-59869-452-
9, ISBN 13: 978-1-59869-452-9.

ISBN 10: 1-4405-8478-8
ISBN 13: 978-1-4405-8478-7
eISBN 10: 1-4405-8479-6
eISBN 13: 978-1-4405-8479-4

Printed in the United States of America.

10 9 8 7 6 5 4 3 2 1

Library of Congress Cataloging-in-Publication Data
Sussman, Lauren, author.
  If I was you . . . / Lauren Sussman.
    pages cm
  Includes index.
  ISBN 978-1-4405-8478-7 (pb) -- ISBN 1-4405-8478-8 (pb) -- ISBN 978-1-4405-
8479-4 (ebook) -- ISBN 1-4405-8479-6 (ebook)
  1. English language--Errors of usage. I. Title.
  PE1460.S89 2014
  428.2--dc23
                          2014030610

Many of the designations used by manufacturers and sellers to distinguish their products
are claimed as trademarks. Where those designations appear in this book and F+W Media,
Inc. was aware of a trademark claim, the designations have been printed with initial capital
letters.

Cover design by Sylvia McArdle.
Cover image © nikoniano/123RF.

*This book is available at quantity discounts for bulk purchases.
For information, please call 1-800-289-0963.*

Contents

INTRODUCTION

If I was you, I'd do something different.

You've probably heard this sentence, or something like it. You may even have used it. Some part of your brain tells you there's something wrong with it, but you're not sure quite what.

There are lots of other sentences like that:

We just saw two baby deers.

The guys vehicle exploded in flames.

Everything's going to be alright now.

Each one of those sentences has something wrong with it, but at first glance the problem may not be obvious. This book is here to show you how to fix these and other incorrect words and sentences. Your guide for this project? The rules of grammar, punctuation, and spelling.

Now, don't let this reference to grammar frighten you. Look at it this way: Grammar is really just a road map to language.

Every time we start to write something, we're setting off on an unknown journey across that big blank computer screen or piece of paper. We usually have a pretty good idea of where we are and where we want to get to. It's the part in between that can be scary.

This is where knowing the basic rules of English grammar and spelling helps. The rules are like signposts at key junctions telling you which way to turn. They help keep you from getting lost and confused amid the strange jungle that is the English language.

That's why you're holding this book. You don't need an exhaustive compilation of all the rules and regulations of our mother tongue. Instead, you want something that's concise and practical—a kind of pocket atlas you can pull out and consult when you feel you've lost your way.

Each of the entries in this book starts with a common mistake. We discuss why the sample sentence is wrong, what point of grammar it illustrates, and how to fix it. Don't worry if a lot of these mistakes sound familiar to you. We're here to help you get your grammar in order and clean up any errors. In the end, you'll have a nice, clear, well-lit, well-signed road in front of you.

You can read the book from beginning to end, but it may be more helpful if you use the index to look up the specific problems about which you have questions. For further information, we've also included a list of resources.

So open your atlas, turn on your GPS, and let's set out on our journey.

Everything's going to be all right now!

[Part I]

Confusing Punctuation Marks (and How to Understand Them)

Wrong: *Hand me the pen that rolled near you*

Misplacing Periods

A period is most often used to signal the end of a sentence that states a fact or one that gives a command or makes a request. For instance, both of the following are simple, declarative sentences that end with periods:

- *The pen fell down right next to your chair.*

- *I'm wondering if it would be that hard for you to bend over and pick it up.*

Although the latter sentence contains an implied question, the end punctuation should be a period because the sentence as a whole states a fact (that I'm wondering something) rather than asks a question. Periods are also used in abbreviations, such as *Dr., Ms., Rev., i.e.,* and *et al.*

Good Grammar Tip

If your declarative or imperative sentence ends with an abbreviation that takes a period, don't put an additional period at the end. Write:

I'll be at your apartment to pick you up at 8 P.M.

not

I'll be at your apartment to pick you up at 8 P.M..

Right: *Hand me the pen that rolled near you.*

Wrong: *Are you available for a long, pointless, late-morning meeting.*

Misused Question Marks

News flash: Question marks go at the end of direct questions and sentences that end in questions. You knew that, didn't you? Couldn't that information have been left out? You get the picture, don't you? Surely the point has sunk in by now, hasn't it?

A question mark is also used to show that there's doubt or uncertainty about something written in a sentence, such as a name, a date, or a word. In birth and death dates, such as (?–1565), the question mark means the birth date hasn't been verified. Look at this example:

- *The police are searching for Richard O. (?) in connection with the crime.*

Here, the question mark means that the author is uncertain about the person's name. But look at this example:

- *He's said to have stolen $5,000 (?) from a children's charity.*

The question mark means that the author is unsure about the exact amount of the theft.

Watch to see if a question mark is part of a title. If it is, be sure to include it in any punctuation that goes with the title:

- *I won't watch that new television program* Can You Believe What Scum These Criminals Are?

Good Grammar Tip

Remember, question marks go inside quotation marks if the quoted material forms a question. Otherwise, question marks go outside quotation marks. Notice the difference in these examples:

Brendan asked, "Who on earth steals money from a kids' charity?"

Did Brendan say, "People like that should be tossed in jail and the key thrown away"?

If you have a series of questions that aren't complete sentences, a question mark should be included after each fragment:

• *Can you believe that it's ten below zero? or that it's snowing? or that my electricity has gone off? or that the freaking electric company hasn't got here to fix the problem?*

Right: *Are you available for a long, pointless, late-morning meeting?*

Wrong: *I can't believe I just won $10 million in the lottery.*

Incorrect Exclamation Points

Another news flash: Exclamation points (exclamation marks) are used to express strong feelings! In the preceding example, unless the speaker has the emotions of a fish, there's a call for something more intense than a period. Exclamation marks add tone and emphasis to a sentence. There's quite a difference between these two sentences:

- *This is the first time I ever bought a lottery ticket.*

- *This is the first time I ever bought a lottery ticket!*

The second sentence tells readers that something quite extraordinary happened when the speaker bought a lottery ticket for the first time.

In formal writing, don't use exclamation points (unless, of course, you're quoting a source or citing a title—or working for a tabloid magazine). In informal writing, you might include exclamation points after information that you find to be remarkable or information that you're excited about:

- *The first thing I'm going to do is donate $5,000 (!) to my favorite charity.*

or

- *The first thing I'm going to do is donate $5,000 to my favorite charity!*

Check to see if an exclamation point is part of a title. If it is, be sure to include it:

- *I wonder if I'll be on that new television program* I Can't Believe They're Millionaires!

On the other hand, it's sometimes easy to go overboard with exclamation points:

- *I met Joan and John for dinner last night! I told them the amazing news! They're so happy for me! They volunteered to go on my Caribbean vacation with me!*

Exciting as this news is (at least to Joan and John), the emotional impact is diminished if every sentence ends with an exclamation point. Use them responsibly.

Good Grammar Tip

Only in informal writing should you use more than one question mark or exclamation mark at a time:

Is this picture of our former roommate for real????

or

I can't believe that our former roommate is featured in Playboy*!!!*

Right: *I can't believe I just won $10 million in the lottery!*

Wrong: *Anna said, Harry, give me the butter, please.*

May I Quote You on That?

Use quotation marks (" ") at the beginning and ending of words, phrases, or sentences to show which words belong to you (the writer) and which belong to someone else.

The most common use of quotation marks is to show readers the exact words a person said, in the exact order the person spoke them. This is called a direct quotation. Note the difference in the following sentences:

- Direct Quotation: *Amber Posey said, "Give me the toast."*
- Indirect Quotation: *Amber Posey said to give her the toast.*
- Direct Quotation: *Carla Fenwick replied, "I don't have the toast."*
- Indirect Quotation: *Carla Fenwick replied that she didn't have the toast.*

The same meaning is conveyed either way, but the quotation marks tell readers the words are written exactly as they were spoken.

One of the most common mistakes that's made with quotation marks is to use them immediately after a word such as *said* or *asked* incorrectly. Quotation marks are used *correctly* in sentences like these:

- *Harry asked, "Anna, will you pass me the butter?"*

- *Anna said, "We don't have any butter."*

The mistake comes in sentences that are **indirect quotations** (that is, the words after *said*, *asked*, and so on aren't the exact words, in the exact order, that the speaker used).

Consider this sentence, which gives the same information about Harry and Anna:

- *Harry asked if Anna would pass him the butter.*

The mistake often made is to punctuate that sentence this way:

- *Harry asked, "If Anna would pass him the butter."*

But the words inside the quotation marks aren't the exact words, in the exact order, that Harry used. Since these aren't the exact words, quotation marks can't be used.

Here are some guidelines to help you use quotation marks correctly:

Guideline 1: Every time you change speakers, indent and start a new paragraph, even if the person quoted is just saying one word. This is the signal for readers to keep straight who's saying what.

Guideline 2: If you're quoting more than one sentence from the same source (a person or a manuscript), put the closing quotation marks at the end of the speaker's last sentence of that paragraph *only*, not at the end of each sentence. This helps readers know that the same person is speaking.

Guideline 3: If you're quoting more than one paragraph from the same source (a person or a manuscript), put beginning quotation marks at the start of each paragraph of your quote and closing quotation marks *only* at the end of the last paragraph. This lets readers know that the words come from the same source, without any interruption.

Guideline 4: Use quotation marks to enclose the titles of short works (short poems, short stories, titles of articles from magazines or newspapers, essays, chapters of books, songs, and episodes of television or radio programs).

Guideline 5: If you're using slang, technical terms, or other expressions outside their normal usage, enclose the words or phrases in quotation marks (alternately, you may put the words or phrases in italics).

Right: *Anna said, "Harry, give me the butter, please."*

Wrong: *I was reading the short story "Scared Out of My Wits",
but I fell asleep in spite of myself.*

Misplaced Punctuation with Quotation Marks

*The rules about placing punctuation in relation to quotation marks may seem a
bit confusing at first, but they really aren't very complicated once you get the hang
of them.*

Periods and commas go *inside* closing quotation marks; colons and
semicolons go *outside* closing quotation marks. Look at this sentence:

- *I was reading the short story "Lights Out," but I fell asleep in spite of myself.*

See the comma after *Out* and before the closing quotation marks?
The actual title of the story is "Lights Out" (there's no comma in the title).
However, the sentence continues and demands a comma, so U.S. English
requires a comma to be placed *inside* the closing quotation marks. Now look
at this sentence:

- *I was reading the short story "Death-Eating Murderous Clowns from the
Hyper-Terror Dimension"; I didn't find it to be scary at all until my friend Jica
unexpectedly tapped me on the shoulder.*

The semicolon is *outside* the closing quotation marks after *Dimension*.
Just to reiterate: the comma goes inside the quotation marks, while the
semicolon goes outside. Okay?

Deciding on placement of the two other end marks of punctuation—the
question mark and the exclamation mark—is tricky: These go either *inside*
or *outside* the closing marks, depending on what's being quoted. Take, for
instance, a question mark. It goes *inside* the closing quotation if what is being
quoted is a question:

- *Jica said, "Was the story really that scary, or are you just a wimp?"*

The words that Jica said form the question, so the question mark goes
inside the closing quotation mark to show readers what she said. Look at this
example:

• *Jica shouted, "I hope you know what you're doing, reading stuff like that late at night!"*

Again, the words that Jica said form the exclamation, so the exclamation mark goes inside the closing quotation mark. Now take a look at this example:

• *Did Jica say, "You must have fallen asleep or you would have heard me come into the room"?*

Note that the words that Jica said (*You must have fallen asleep or you would have heard me come into the room*) don't form a question; the sentence as a whole does. The question mark goes *outside* the closing quotation marks to show readers that.

• *"No, I actually said, 'You must be right'!"*

Again, the words that you said don't form an exclamation; the sentence as a whole does (probably expressing irritation). The exclamation mark goes *outside* the single quotation marks to show readers that.

Good Grammar Tip

If a quoted sentence is interrupted by words such as *he said* or *she replied*, use commas in this way:

"For this contest," he said, "you need three pencils and two pieces of paper."

The first comma goes before the closing quotation mark and the second comma goes before the beginning quotation mark.

If the words being quoted make up a question or an exclamation, don't include a comma:

"Put that down right now!" Barry cried.

What do you do when both the sentence as a whole *and* the words being quoted form a question or an exclamation? Use only *one* end mark (question mark or exclamation mark) and put it *inside* the closing quotation marks. Look at this example:

- *Did I hear Jica say, "Who reads that kind of stuff anyway?"*

Right: *I was reading the short story "Scared Out of My Wits," but I fell asleep in spite of myself.*

Wrong: *"Mark Lester said, "I'll be fine," but then he collapsed," cried Marrin Wright.*

Incorrect Quotes Within Quotes

In the United States, single quotation marks are used for a quotation within a quotation:

• *"He was reading the story 'Plaid Blazers and Other Mysteries,'" said Tara Hoggard.*

Do you see that what Mark said (*I'll be fine*) and the name of the short story (*Plaid Blazers and Other Mysteries*) would normally be enclosed with double quotation marks? But since these phrases come inside material that's already in double marks, you show readers where the quotation (or title) begins by using a single quotation mark.

Note that the comma following *fine* and *Mysteries* comes inside the single quotation mark. Some styles prefer a space between the single and double quotations when they occur together (as at the end of the second sentence). Check whatever style guide you're using to be sure what's required.

When should you not use quotation marks with quotes? If you're using the writing guidelines from the Modern Language Association (MLA) or the American Psychological Association (APA), keep in mind that these groups have specific rules for block quotations (passages of a certain length). In spite of the fact that you're quoting, you don't use quotation marks. You do, however, have a definite format for letting readers know that the material you're citing is verbatim from the original text. Consult the specific guidelines for each group to see how to format this material.

Right: *"Mark Lester said, 'I'll be fine,' but then he collapsed," cried Marrin Wright.*

Wrong: *The guys vehicle exploded in flames.*

Wrong Possessive Apostrophe

Before using an apostrophe to show possession, first make sure the phrase in question actually denotes possession and isn't simply a plural. For instance, in the phrase the guy's vehicle, *one guy possesses a vehicle (so an apostrophe before the* s *indicates this to readers); however, in the phrase* the guys in their vehicles, *the guys aren't possessing anything and an apostrophe isn't needed.*

Here are some guidelines to help you make sense of it all.

Guideline 1: *If a singular noun doesn't end in* -s, *its possessive ends in* -'s. *Say what? Take a look at this sentence:*

- *Despite the flames, the cars engine was still running.*

The word *cars* needs an apostrophe to indicate possession, but where does the apostrophe go?

Use this mental trick: Take the word that needs the apostrophe (*cars*) and the word that it's talking about (*engine*) and mentally turn the two words around so that the word you're wondering about is the object of a preposition. (This rule may be easier for you to understand this way: Turn the words around so that they form a phrase. Usually the phrase will use *of, from,* or *belonging to.*)

When you change *cars engine* around, you come up with *engine of the car.* Now look at the word *car. Car* is singular and doesn't end in -*s,* so the original should be punctuated -*'s.* You should have:

- *Despite the flames, the car's engine was still running.*

Try the trick again with this sentence:

- *Donna Moores wallet was lying on the car seat.*

Mentally turn *Donna Moores wallet* around so that you have *the wallet of (belonging to) Donna Moore.* After you've turned it around, you have the words *Donna Moore,* which is singular (in spite of being two words) and doesn't end in -*s.* That lets you know that you need to use -*'s.* The sentence should be punctuated this way:

- *Donna Moore's wallet was lying on the car seat.*

And we certainly hope she recovered it safely.

Guideline 2: *When you have plural nouns that end in -s (and most do), add an apostrophe after the final -s. This tells readers that you're talking about several people, places, or things. The same mental trick of turning the two words into a phrase applies.*

This sentence talks about two girls who had been reported missing:

- *The girls coats were completely destroyed by the fire.*

Now just apply the trick. Take the phrase *girls coats*, and turn it around so that you have *coats of (belonging to) the girls.*

When you've turned the phrase around this time, the word *girls* ends in -*s*. This lets you know that you should add an apostrophe after the -*s* in *girls*, so the sentence is punctuated this way:

- *The girls' coats were completely destroyed by the fire.*

Although most English plurals end in -*s* or -*es*, our language has a number of exceptions (and didn't you know there would be?), such as *children, women,* and *deer*. If a plural doesn't end in -*s*, the possessive is formed with an -*'s* (that is, treat it as if it were singular).

Again, the turnaround trick applies. Take the sentence:

- *The childrens coats, however, were outside the vehicle and so were saved.*

Mentally turn *childrens coats* into the phrase *coats of the children*. Since *children* doesn't end in -*s*, its possessive would be -*'s*; so the correct punctuation would be:

- *The children's coats were covered with mud.*

So far, so good? You have just one tricky part left to consider. It concerns singular words that end in -*s*. Two ways of punctuating these words are common, as follows.

Guideline 3: *First, if a singular word ends in -s, form its possessive by adding -'s (except in situations in which pronunciation would be difficult, such as* Moses *or* Achilles*). Look at this sentence:*

- *Julie Jones information was invaluable in locating the right insurance company.*

Applying the turnaround trick would make the phrase that needs the apostrophe read this way: *information from Julie Jones.*

The rule just mentioned would tell you that, since *Jones* is singular and ends in -*s*, you'd form the possessive by adding -*'s*. Therefore, the sentence would be punctuated this way:

• *Julie Jones's information was invaluable in locating the right insurance company.*

However, you may be told to use another rule:

Guideline 4: *If a singular word ends in* -s, *form its possessive by adding an apostrophe after the* -s. *In this case, the sentence would be written this way:*

• *Julie Jones' information was invaluable in locating the right insurance company.*

If using this alternate rule is okay with your teacher or employer, then you have to remember only two rules about placing the apostrophe in possessives:

1.   After you mentally turn the phrase around, if the word in question doesn't end in -*s*, add -*'s*.

2.   After you mentally turn the phrase around, if the word in question ends in -*s*, add an apostrophe after the -*s*.

Good Grammar Tip

One of the most common grammatical errors involving apostrophes is the incorrect use of *it's* and *its*.

Actually, the rule governing this is pretty simple: *Its* is the possessive form and doesn't take an apostrophe; *it's* is *only* used as a contraction, meaning *it is*. Also remember that all **possessive pronouns** (*its, yours, his, hers, theirs, ours, whose*) *never* take an apostrophe.

One use of apostrophes shows readers whether the people you're talking about possess (own) something jointly or individually. Take a look at this sentence:

• *Jim and Allisons cars were stolen.*

The question is, did Jim and Allison own the cars together or separately? If, say, Jim and Allison were a couple and they had the misfortune of having two of their cars stolen, then the sentence would be punctuated this way:

- *Jim and Allison's cars were stolen.*

The possessive comes after the last person's name *only*. This usage tells readers that Jim and Allison had joint ownership of the cars.

But maybe Jim and Allison were neighbors, and a rash of car thefts had taken place on their block. The sentence would then be punctuated this way:

- *Jim's and Allison's cars were stolen.*

The possessive comes after *both* names. This tells readers that Jim and Allison had separate ownership of the cars.

Right: *The guy's vehicle exploded in flames.*

Wrong: *The best thing's in life are free.*

Misunderstood Plurals with Apostrophes

Next time you're out walking around, take a look at some store signs. I guarantee that you'll see some like these:

- *Special price's this week!*

- *Rent two movie's today!*

- *Five can's for $4.00!*

The words that have apostrophes are just plain ol' plurals; they don't show ownership in any way and so don't need apostrophes. (If you're unsure about whether you should use an apostrophe, ask yourself if the word in question owns or possesses anything.)

Also, if you have proverbial expressions that involve individual letters or combinations of letters, use apostrophes to show their plurals.

- *Dot your i's and cross your t's.*

In these examples, some academic or company style guides dictate that you shouldn't italicize the letter you're making plural; other guides take the opposite view. Be sure to consult the guide suggested by your instructor or company.

Another time that you should use an apostrophe to form a plural is if your reader would be confused by reading an *-s* alone (for instance, when an *-s* is added to an individual letter or letter combination or to numbers used as nouns).

s = s's (instead of ss)

Write 7's (instead of 7s) in the graph.

Right: *The best things in life are free.*

Wrong: *Shell be comin round the mountain when she comes.*

Messed-Up Contractions

An apostrophe often indicates that at least one letter has been omitted from a word, and the word that's formed is called a contraction. For example, the contraction don't *stands for* do not; *the* o *in* not *has been omitted.* I'll *is a short form of* I will; *in this case the* wi *of* will *has been omitted.*

Do you know the contractions formed from these words?

she will	she'll
you have	you've
he is	he's

Contractions can also replace words such as *would*:

- *You'd have thought she'd have gotten here by this time.*

That sentence could also be written more formally:

- *You would have thought she would have gotten here by this time.*

Have is also occasionally replaced by a contraction, as in the following sentence:

- *I guess I could 'a gone to meet her.*

Good Grammar Tip

Sometimes authors will use apostrophes in contractions to help readers understand dialect. For instance, someone might say, "We'll go skinny dippin' down by the creek." Readers understand that the final g is omitted from *dipping*, and that the author is trying to duplicate the type of speech (the dialect) a character uses.

Right: *She'll be comin' round the mountain when she comes.*

Wrong: *Jeff dedicated his book to his parents*
God and Henry Kissinger.

How Not to Use Serial Commas

If you have a series of items, use a comma to separate the items. Take a look at this sentence:

• *Jeff's parents God and Henry Kissinger were all important influences on his writing.*

How many people were influencing Jeff here? With the following punctuation, you'd see two people (well, one person and one deity, really) were involved:

• *Jeff's parents, God and Henry Kissinger, were all important influences on his writing.*

However, the following punctuation shows that two people and the deity were involved—which is probably what Jeff meant in his dedication:

• *Jeff's parents, God, and Henry Kissinger were all important influences on his writing.*

Use a comma between two or more adjectives (words that explain or describe or give more information about a noun or pronoun) that modify a noun (the name of a person, place, thing, or idea):

• *Jeff's book is brilliant, comprehensive, and far-seeing.*

If the first adjective modifies the idea expressed by the combination of subsequent adjectives and the noun, then you don't need commas. Look at this sentence:

• *Among his themes is the importance of stable central governments in the modern Middle East.*

Since *central governments* would be considered a single unit, you don't need to separate it from the adjective modifying it (*stable*) with a comma.

If you're using *and, or,* or *nor* to connect all the items in the series, don't use commas:

• *Jeff's admirers are wealthy and educated and literate.*

• *His readers might be private citizens or public officials or political professionals.*

• *The book is neither easy nor reassuring nor banal.*

Good Grammar Tip

Some style guides mandate that the final two items in a series (also referred to as the "serial comma," "Harvard comma," or "Oxford comma") always be separated by commas; other guides dictate that it be eliminated, except in cases where the meaning would be misconstrued without it. You should find out which style your instructor or company prefers.

Right: *Jeff dedicated his book to his parents, God, and Henry Kissinger.*

Wrong: *We'd been sitting in the restaurant for a long time, and wanted our lunch.*

Wrong Use of Commas in a Compound Sentence

If you have two independent clauses (that is, two thoughts that could stand alone as sentences) and they're joined by but, or, yet, so, for, and, *or* nor *(use the mnemonic* boysfan *to help you remember), join them with a comma:*

- *It was more than three hours past lunchtime, and everybody was grumbling about being hungry.*

In the sentence at the beginning of this section, though, *and wanted our lunch* isn't an independent clause; it can't stand alone as a sentence. Therefore, the comma before it is unnecessary and incorrect.

There's an exception to this rule about joining two or more independent clauses with commas: You may eliminate the comma if the two independent clauses are short and if the sentence would still be clear without the comma. For example:

- *John and Julia stood and they said they were walking out.*

If you have a simple sentence with a compound verb, don't put a comma between the verbs:

- *I wanted food as well but felt we should be patient and wait for the rest of the group.*

Good Grammar Tip

Avoid using a comma with words that are generally thought of as pairs—even if they're in a series. For instance, you'd write:

I ate an apple, an orange, and peanut butter and jelly every day in grade school.

Right: *We'd been sitting in the restaurant for a long time and wanted our lunch.*

Wrong: *Hey that hunk sitting over there the
one with the blue eyes he's gorgeous!*

Problems Involving Commas with Clauses, Phrases, Appositives, and Introductory Words

Use commas to set apart clauses (groups of words that have a subject and a predicate), participle phrases, and appositives (words or phrases that give information about a noun or pronoun) that aren't necessary to the meaning of the sentence.

Take a look at this sentence:

• *The to-die-for man over there, the only one who works in the deli at Sam's Supermarket, has black hair and brown eyes.*

If you took out the clause *the only one who works in the deli at Sam's Supermarket*, you'd still have the same essential parts of the sentence. You don't need to know where the man works in order to learn his hair and eye color. (The nonessential part of this sentence is called a nonrestrictive clause.) Here's another way of looking at it: If you can take out the part in question (the part you're questioning for commas) and the sentence still makes sense, then you should use the commas. Now look:

• *The only man who works in the deli at Sam's Supermarket was arrested for stealing four grapes and five apples.*

In this case, if you removed *who works in the deli at Sam's Supermarket*, you'd have *The only man was arrested for stealing four grapes and five apples.* That isn't the meaning of the original sentence. Remember: If you need the extra words for the meaning, you don't need the commas.

Commas are also used after **introductory words** such as exclamations, common expressions, and names used in direct address that aren't necessary for the meaning of a sentence. If you have words that begin a sentence and you can understand the sentence without them, use a comma to separate them from the rest of the sentence. For example:

• *Why, don't you look nice tonight!*

- *Now, did you remember to bring your pepper spray?*

- *If you must know, I have been dyeing my hair for the past ten years.*

A comma is also used before these same types of words and phrases when they appear at the end of a sentence, as long as they're not necessary for the meaning:

- *Don't you think these shoes make me look three inches taller, Madison?*

- *You're not going to the party dressed like that, are you?*

- *Go back to your bedroom and put on something decent, if you please.*

Use commas around words that interrupt a sentence (these words are called **parenthetical expressions**), as long as the words aren't necessary for the meaning:

- *The answer to your question, Paula, is yes, I asked, and he's divorced.*

- *This time, unlike the previous twelve dates, I'm not going to let him drive me home.*

Use a comma after an introductory **verbal** (a verbal is a participle, gerund, or infinitive) or verbal phrase:

- *Almost weeping at the sight of his bare chest, Allison excused herself and went into the next room to recover.*

- *To try to regain her composure, she took several deep breaths.*

Use a comma after an introductory **adverb clause**. (An adverb clause is a group of words that has a subject and a verb, and describes a verb, adjective, or other adverb.) For example:

- *Because Allison wasn't thinking clearly, she spent the next twenty-four hours feeling guilty.*

• *If he shows up in the bar tonight, I'm going to completely ignore him.*

To come back to our first sentence, *hey* is an introductory word and so is separated from the rest of the sentence with a comma, *the one with the blue eyes* is appositive to *that hunk sitting over there*, and finally *he's gorgeous* is an independent clause.

Right: *Hey, that hunk sitting over there,
the one with the blue eyes, he's gorgeous!*

Wrong: *To Mr. Ralph Trautstein 319 First Avenue New York NY 10031*

Erroneous Commas in Dates, Addresses, and Letters

When writing out a mailing address as text (not on separate lines), put a comma between the person's last name and the start of the street address, then after the street address, then between the city and the state. Don't put a comma between the state and the zip code. For example:

• *Please remit the payment to Cooper Bartlett, 4238 Old Highway 41 North, Nicholasville, KY 42309.*

If you're putting address information on separate lines, use a comma only between the city and state:

• *Cooper Bartlett*

• *4238 Old Highway 41 North*

• *Nicholasville, KY 42356.*

If you mention a city and state in text, put commas around the state:

• *I have to visit Clinton, Iowa, on my next sales trip.*

The same is true if you mention a city and country; put commas around the country:

• *For my next business trip, I have to visit Bangalore, India, to inspect one of our factories.*

Put a comma after the day of the week (if you've stated it), the day of the month, and the year (if the sentence continues):

• *John Abbott will meet you on Friday, February 22, 2008, at 7:30 A.M.*

If you're writing only the day and month or the month and year, no comma is necessary:

- *John Abbott will meet you on February 22.*

- *John Abbott will meet you in February 2008.*

Put a comma after the greeting (salutation) of all friendly letters and the closing of all letters:

- *Dear Aunt Helen,*

- *Sincerely,*

Right: *To Mr. Ralph Trautstein, 319 First Avenue, New York, NY 10031*

Wrong: *Please call Robert Housholder PhD at your convenience to discuss the $2000 payment.*

Wrong Commas in Degrees, Titles, and Long Numbers

Many people use academic or professional titles with their names, especially in formal communication. If a person's title or degree follows his or her name, put commas after or around it:

- *Please call Robert Housholder, PhD, at your convenience.*

- *The deposition was given by Edward Shuttleworth, MD.*

Good Grammar Tip

A mistake that seems to be cropping up more and more is using a comma to separate a verb from its subject (as in "The flour, had been infested with bugs"). The comma after *flour* should be eliminated.

When it comes to numbers, your goal is clarity, especially when the number is a big one. Using commas helps readers understand long numbers more easily. If, for instance, you read the number *1376993*, you'd have to stop, count the numbers, and then group them in threes before you could understand the number. Using commas to divide the numbers makes for quicker interpretation:

- *Is it my imagination, or does this book list 1,376,993 rules for commas?*

Just remember that it's one comma for every three digits, starting from the right.

Right: *Please call Robert Housholder, PhD, at your convenience to discuss the $2,000 payment.*

Wrong: *For the whitewater rafting trip, you'll need these things, a bathing suit, a life jacket, a canoe paddle, and some shark repellent.*

Misplaced Colons

Use a colon to introduce particular information. One of the most common uses of a colon is to signal to readers that a list will follow:

• *On the camping trip, please bring the following: a flashlight, a sleeping bag, two boxes of matches, and food for six meals.*

Good Grammar Tip

If you have a list that is the object of a verb or of a preposition, you don't need a colon:

On the camping trip, please bring a flashlight, a sleeping bag, two boxes of matches, and food for six meals.

(The list is the object of the verb *bring*.)

On the camping trip, please bring your supplies to Tom, Sally, Mykela, or Fernando.

(The list is the object of the preposition *to*.)

To be on the safe side, use an expression such as *the following* or *as follows* before a colon.

You can also use a colon to explain or give more information about what has come before it in a sentence:

• *I have a number of complaints against the other campers: loud music late at night, stealing supplies from us, and littering the campsite.*

In formal papers, a colon usually precedes a lengthy quotation:

- *The campground guide states: "All radios and CD players must be turned off or played with headphones after 10 P.M. There are no exceptions to this rule. Please respect the privacy of your fellow nature lovers."*

To determine what is meant by "lengthy," consult the style guide designated by your instructor or employer.

Here are other times to use a colon:

- In the greeting of a business letter (*To Whom It May Concern:*)
- Between the hour and minutes in time (*a meeting at 4:15 P.M.*)
- In dividing a title from its subtitle (*My Favorite Punctuation Marks: Why I Love Colons*)
- In naming a chapter and verse of the Bible (*Genesis 2:10*)
- In naming the volume and number of a magazine (*TIME 41:14*)
- In citing the volume and page number of a magazine (*U.S. News & World Report 166: 31*)
- Between the city and the publisher in a bibliographical entry (*London: Covent Garden Press*)

Right: *For the whitewater rafting trip, you'll need these things: a bathing suit, a life jacket, a canoe paddle, and some shark repellent.*

Wrong: *John Wilson went into the bank to rob it; using counterfeit money.*

Wrong Use of Semicolons

> *I have grown fond of semicolons in recent years . . . . It is almost always a greater pleasure to come across a semicolon than a period.*
> —Lewis Thomas, MD, from *The Medusa and the Snail*

Although most people probably don't get as excited over semicolons as award-winning author and scientist Mr. Thomas did, these punctuation marks can be very useful in their own way.

Semicolons signal a pause greater than one indicated by a comma but less than one indicated by a period. The most common use for a semicolon is joining two complete thoughts (independent clauses) into one sentence. It's particularly important that both clauses be complete thoughts, each with a subject and a predicate. This is where most semicolon users fall down.

Look at the following sentences:

• *The bank teller determined the bill was counterfeit. No serial number was on it.*

Each of these sentences stands alone, but they could be joined by a semicolon:

• *The bank teller determined the bill was counterfeit; no serial number was on it.*

Good Grammar Tip

Remember the mnemonic *boysfan* (the words *but, only, yet, so, for, and,* and *nor*)? If you join complete thoughts with one of those words, use a comma instead of a semicolon.

Often semicolons are used with conjunctive adverbs and other transitional words or phrases, such as *on the other hand* or *therefore*. In this case, be sure that you put the semicolon at the point where the two thoughts are separated.

Semicolons are sometimes used at the end of bulleted or numbered lists, depending on the style and the sentence construction. (Sometimes commas or periods are used, and sometimes there's no punctuation at all.) The important thing is to be consistent. A list may appear like this:

• *In order to make a court case against John Wilson, the prosecution needed to do the following:*

1. *confirm that Wilson knew the money was counterfeit;*
2. *prove that he knowingly tried to defraud the bank;*
3. *establish that he made his plans beforehand.*

Good Grammar Tip

In English, many transitional words and phrases are commonly used. Here are a few of them:

first	second	third
next	finally	then
moreover	likewise	similarly
for instance	nevertheless	consequently
otherwise	instead	as a result
that is	namely	in addition

Now it's time to break a rule about semicolons. Sometimes you use a semicolon when a comma might seem to be the correct punctuation mark. Look at this sentence:

• *The manhunt took place in Los Angeles, Nashville, Indiana, Stratford, Connecticut, Enid, Oklahoma, Dallas, and Olympia.*

Commas came after the name of each city and each state, as the rule on commas says they should. However, readers will probably be confused about the true meaning of the sentence. Consider that a semicolon is a "notch above" a comma. By substituting a semicolon in places where you'd ordinarily use a comma, you make the material clearer for readers by showing which cities go with which states. Look at how the sentence should be punctuated:

- *The manhunt took place in Los Angeles; Nashville, Indiana; Stratford, Connecticut; Enid, Oklahoma; Dallas; and Olympia.*

Reading the sentence with semicolons used in this way, readers can tell that the manhunt took place in Nashville, Indiana, as opposed to Nashville, Tennessee. Also, readers can identify that Enid is located in Oklahoma.

All of this isn't to say that you should always use semicolons. Sometimes you just need to stay away from them. Semicolons won't work if the two thoughts aren't on the same playing field (that is, if they're not logically connected). Look at these two sentences:

- *The teller wore a blue suit. The police responded immediately.*

Although both are sentences, they have no logical link. If a semicolon were used between these two sentences, readers would be scratching their heads, thinking they were missing something.

Semicolons also won't work if one of the thoughts isn't a complete sentence. Look at this example:

- *The police came immediately; screeching through the streets.*

The first part of the sentence is a complete thought (*the police came immediately*), but the second part isn't (*screeching through the streets*).

Regarding the sample sentence at the start of this section, we could turn the semicolon into a comma:

- *John Wilson went into the bank to rob it, using counterfeit money.*

However, we would need to add some information to make the material after the semicolon an independent clause.

Right: *John Wilson went into the bank to rob it; using counterfeit money was, he thought, the best strategy.*

> **Wrong:** *Lindsay thought her mom was a tyr-*
> *ant with an over protective attitude.*

Incorrect Use of Hyphens

Hyphens and dashes are another tricky punctuation pair. A hyphen is a short horizontal line (next to a zero on a keyboard); a dash is longer. But the differences between them go much deeper than just a few fractions of an inch.

The most common use of the hyphen is to divide words at the ends of lines. The important rule to remember is that you may divide words only between syllables. Why is this important, you ask? Read the following lines:

• *Sarah was unhappy with her oldest child, her nineteen-year-old da-ughter Lindsay. Lindsay was still relying on her mother to get her up wh-en the alarm clock rang in the mornings, to see that her various deadli-nes for typing papers for school were met, to take her side in the cons-tant squabbles with her boyfriend, Harry.*

See how difficult this is to read? That's because you've learned to read in syllables. When words aren't divided correctly, readers have to go back to the previous line and put the syllables together, and that's confusing and time-consuming.

The text should read:

• *Sarah was unhappy with her oldest child, her nineteen-year-old daugh-ter Lindsay. Lindsay was still relying on her mother to get her up when the alarm clock rang in the mornings, to see that her various dead-lines for typing papers for school were met, and to take her side in the con-stant squabbles with her boyfriend, Harry.*

If you're not sure where syllables occur, consult a dictionary. In addition, most word-processing software contains automatic hyphenation tools you may use. Since you may divide a word only between its syllables, one-syllable words may not be divided.

No matter where the words are divided, be careful to leave more than one letter at the end of a line (or more than two at the beginning of a line) so that readers' eyes can adjust quickly.

You wouldn't write:

• *Lindsay wondered if the employment agency would call her back a-gain for another interview.*

Nor would you write:

• *Lindsay killed her chances for another interview when she contact-ed the company president by telephone.*

You should also avoid hyphenating acronyms (such as *UNESCO* or *NAACP*), numerals (such as *1,200* or *692*), and contractions (such as *haven't, didn't, couldn't*). Some style guides say that proper nouns (those that are capitalized) shouldn't be hyphenated.

Also try to avoid dividing an Internet or e-mail address. Since these addresses often contain hyphens as part of the address, inserting an extra hyphen would certainly confuse readers. If angle brackets aren't used, extending the address to the second line without any extra punctuation would make the address clear for your reader. You should do that this way:

• *When Lindsay tried to look for more job opportunities, she was directed to:* www.nigerianchanceforfreemoney.com

Use a dash (not a hyphen) between two dates and between two page numbers:

• *Prohibition (1920–1933) came about as a result of the Eighteenth Amendment.*

• *See the section on the Roaring Twenties (pp. 31–35) for more information.*

Good Grammar Tip

Technically, both of the instances referred to use what's called an en dash, which is longer than a hyphen and shorter than a normal dash, which is usually called an em dash. Are you confused? Don't be. Most word-processing programs have an insert icon or a character map that you can use to access en and em dashes, as well as other symbols.

Another common use of the hyphen comes when numbers are written as words instead of numerals. You probably do this already, but the rule says to hyphenate numbers from twenty-one to ninety-nine. If you look at words printed without a hyphen (e.g., *sixtyfour*, *eightyseven*), you see that they're difficult to read. Using hyphens makes reading easier.

Hyphens with Compound Adjectives

When a compound adjective (two or more adjectives that go together to form one thought or image) precedes the noun it modifies, it should be hyphenated. Look at these sentences:

• *Lindsay's boyfriend, Harry, was a long-time employee of a software company.*

In this case, *long-time* is an adjective (it modifies the noun *employee*), and so it's hyphenated. Notice the difference:

• *Lindsay's boyfriend, Harry, had worked for the software company a long time.*

Here, *long time* follows but does not precede the noun it's modifying.

Use a hyphen to join adjectives only if together they form the image. If they're separate words describing a noun (as in *big, bulky package*), then don't use a hyphen. Take a look at this example:

• *loyal, ever-ready friend*

Ever and *ready* go together to form the image that describes the friend, so they're hyphenated. If the hyphen wasn't there, then readers would see *ever ready friend* and would wonder what an *ever friend* was.

Good Grammar Tip

If a modifier before a noun is the word *very* or is an adverb that ends in *-ly*, you don't need a hyphen. You should write:

a very condescending attitude	*a strictly guarded secret*
a very little amount of money	*the highly publicized meeting*

Sometimes you should use a hyphen to clarify the meaning of your sentence. For instance, look at this example:

- *My favorite sports star resigned!*

Should you be elated or upset? The way the sentence is punctuated now, the star will no longer play; his or her fans will be upset. If, however, the writer intended to get across that the star had signed another contract, the sentence should contain a hyphen and be written this way:

- *My favorite sports star re-signed!*

Now you understand the writer's intent. Not many words have this idiosyncrasy (*recreation* and *recollect* are two others), but be careful of those that do.

Good Grammar Tip

Hyphens are often only needed with three prefixes (*ex-*, *self-*, and *all-*) and only with one suffix (*-elect*). Also, any time a prefix comes before a capitalized word, the prefix is hyphenated (such as *anti-American*). This is to avoid a capital letter in the middle of a word.

Right: *Lindsay thought her mom was a tyrant with an overprotective attitude.*

Wrong: *The mechanic told me my car—which I brought in for service last week was fixed.*

Bad Dashes

Ah, the "playful" dash. It provides a window for some informality in writing, allowing the writer to introduce an abrupt change in thought or tone. Look at this sentence:

> • *The odometer just reached thirty thousand miles, so it's time to call the garage for—oops! I just passed the street where we were supposed to turn.*

The dash tells readers that a sudden idea interrupted the speaker's original thought.

Good Grammar Tip

A dash shouldn't be preceded or followed by an extra space.

Use a dash to give emphasis to something that's come before. Look at this sentence:

> • *Elizabeth spent many hours planning what she would pack in the van—the van that broke down ten minutes after she left home.*

Another time a dash may be used is in defining or giving more information about something in a sentence. Read this sentence:

> • *Elizabeth had the van towed to the garage—the place where she'd received such poor auto service.*

The last example could also be punctuated by using parentheses in place of the dash. You might have written the same sentence this way:

> • *Elizabeth had the van towed to the garage (the place where she'd received such poor auto service).*

You can also use a colon to perform the same function. For example:

• *Elizabeth had the van towed to the garage: the place where she'd received such poor auto service.*

However, punctuating the sentence with colons is much stuffier than using a dash or parentheses. Generally speaking, save the colon for formal writing. With the dash you can enjoy yourself a bit more! (Elizabeth, on the other hand, is probably not enjoying herself one bit.)

Good Grammar Tip

Be careful not to overuse dashes. If you do, they lose their effectiveness, and your writing looks too conversational or amateurish.

Finally, you can use a pair of dashes to separate out information in the sentence that adds to but isn't essential to its meaning. In this case, you should be able to remove the material enclosed by the dashes without changing the meaning of the original sentence. For instance:

• *Peter was pretty sure that the mechanic's negligence—which had caused his engine to fail after only a day—should be brought to the attention of the garage owner.*

Here, if we took out the clause surrounded by dashes, the sentence would read:

• *Peter was pretty sure that the mechanic's negligence should be brought to the attention of the garage owner.*

This is still a coherent thought and doesn't change the basic meaning of the original sentence. The dash-surrounded clause just enhances that meaning.

Right: *The mechanic told me my car—which I brought in for service last week—was fixed.*

Wrong: *In the movie* Psycho, *Alfred Hitchcock who was (America's greatest filmmaker) brought to the screen a protagonist who dies less than halfway through the movie.*

Wrong Placement of Parentheses

You know what parentheses are (and in case some smart aleck asks you, the singular of the word is parenthesis and the plural is parentheses), but you may not be completely sure of when and how to use them. The following sections should help you master this punctuation in a matter of minutes.

Using parentheses tells readers that you're giving some extra information, something that isn't necessary to the meaning of the sentence but is helpful in understanding what's being read. For example:

• *For a complete study of Hitchcock's movies, consult Chapter 8 (pages 85–96).*

When readers see parentheses, they know that the material enclosed is extraneous to the meaning of the sentence. If the information is necessary for the sentence to be read correctly, you shouldn't use parentheses. For instance you might write the following sentence:

• *Among Hitchcock's most famous films are* Psycho *(1960) and* The Birds *(1963).*

You can use parentheses to set off the dates of the films because in this context they aren't essential to the sentence's meaning. However, suppose you were to write:

• *Hitchcock's 1960 film* Psycho *anticipates many of images he would use in his 1963 masterpiece* The Birds.

In this sentence, the dates are an important element of your point—the fact that *Psycho* came before *The Birds* is key to understanding what you're saying. So you can't set off the dates with parentheses.

To take another example, you can write a sentence like this:

• *I haven't recovered from my latest (and, I hope, my last) adventure with blind dates at movies.*

You could omit the material inside the parentheses and you'd still have the essence of the sentence. Granted, the sentence wouldn't be as cleverly worded, but the gist would be the same.

Good Grammar Tip

If you need punctuation with the material inside the parentheses, place the punctuation marks inside the parentheses. Look at this sentence:

If someone wants to learn about the films of Alfred Hitchcock (and who wouldn't?), he or she would ask me because I'm an expert.

Only the words *and who wouldn't* form the question, and they're inside the parentheses, so the question mark also goes there.

Another time parentheses are commonly used is in citing dates, especially birth and death dates:

• *Alfred Hitchcock (1899–1980) directed more than fifty films over a half century.*

In addition, use parentheses to enclose numbers or letters that name items in a series. Sometimes both the parentheses marks are used, and sometimes just the mark on the right-hand side is used:

• *Before going to an Alfred Hitchcock film with me, you should (a) buy popcorn; (b) read something about Hitchcock so you won't sound ignorant; (c) prepare to be instructed.*

• *Before talking to me about Hitchcock, you should a) know what you're talking about; b) assume I know more; c) not say anything.*

Whether you use both parentheses or just one, be consistent. Also, be aware that if you use one parenthesis only, your reader may easily get the letter mixed up with the preceding word.

In material that covers politics, you'll often see parentheses used to give a legislator's party affiliation and home state (in the case of national politics) or city or county (in the case of state politics). For example:

- *Senator Willa Liberi (D-R.I.) met in her Washington office with a number of colleagues, including Representative Mark Digery (R-Providence).*

Another—though less common—use for parentheses is to show readers that an alternate ending for a word may be read. Take a look at this sentence:

- *Please bring your child(ren) to the company picnic.*

Keep in mind that parentheses would not be used this way in more formal writing; the sentence would be reworded to include both *child* and *children*.

Right: *In the movie* Psycho, *Alfred Hitchcock (who was America's greatest filmmaker) brought to the screen a protagonist who dies less than halfway through the movie.*

Wrong: *"He, Justin, [was very late] to his own birthday party but didn't even apologize."*

Incorrect Brackets

Ordinarily, square brackets aren't used very often, except in dictionaries. A detailed dictionary will often use brackets to show the etymology, or the history, of the word being defined. (Now be honest—you've never noticed brackets in dictionaries, have you?)

One use of square brackets is to make certain that quoted material is clear or understandable for readers. Suppose you're quoting a sentence that contains a pronoun without its antecedent, as in this example:

- *"He burst into the party and was completely obnoxious."*

Just who is *he?* Unless the previous sentences had identified him, readers wouldn't know. In that case, you'd use square brackets this way:

- *"He [Justin Lake] burst into the party and was completely obnoxious."*

Here's another example:

- *"It came as a big surprise to everyone at the party."*

Readers would have no idea what *it* was. An announcement of retirement? An unexpected large check? A stripper popping out of a cake?

To explain the pronoun so that readers understand the material more clearly, you might use brackets in this way:

- *"It [Justin's behavior] came as a big surprise to everyone at the party."*

Along the same lines, you use brackets to alter the capitalization of something you're quoting so that it fits in your sentence or paragraph. For example:

- *"[T]he guests began to exit rapidly when Justin became uncontrollably drunk."*

Use brackets for quoted material only if their use doesn't change the meaning of what's being quoted.

Good Grammar Tip

Remember! Just as with love and marriage and that horse and carriage, you can't have one side of parentheses or brackets without the other (except in display lists).

Another time that brackets are used occurs even less frequently. If you need to give information that you'd normally put in parentheses—but that information is already in parentheses—use brackets instead. This may sound confusing, but take a look at this and you'll see how the rule applies:

• *The man responsible for Justin's arrest (James Bradson [1958–2013]) was never given credit.*

Normally, you put a person's birth and death dates in parentheses, but since those dates are placed in material that's already in parentheses, you use brackets instead.

Good Grammar Tip

Depending on the type of writing you do, you might add the Latin word *sic* to the information that you're quoting. You don't know what *sic* means? *Sic* shows that what you're quoting has a mistake that you're copying. By seeing the *sic* designation, readers know that the mistake was made by the original author and not you. Look at this sentence:

"This painting was donated to the museum on September 31 [sic]."

Now, you know and I know that "thirty days hath September"—not thirty-one, as stated in the example. By using [sic] readers can tell that you copied the mistake as it was written in the original form. Note that *sic* is enclosed in brackets (many handbooks or style guides dictate that it be italicized as well).

Most style guides allow you to use either brackets or parentheses to let readers know that you've added italics to quoted material. The only rule is that you keep using the same choice of punctuation throughout the manuscript. Take your pick:

- *"The time of the arrest is as equally important as is the date [emphasis added]."*

- *"The time of the arrest is as equally important as is the date (emphasis added)."*

This lets readers know that you—not the original speaker or writer—inserted the italics to emphasize specific material.

Generally speaking, you'll use brackets rarely—unless you're writing in a particular style. For example, in writing a script, stage directions are generally enclosed in brackets. As with any writing, if you're told to use a particular style guide (say, for instance, *The Chicago Manual of Style*), consult it for the other infrequent times that brackets are used.

Before Internet usage became so commonplace, you'd see angle brackets used only in a mathematical context, with > being the symbol for *greater than* and < being the symbol for *less than*.

Today, however, angle brackets are often used before and after URLs. Using angle brackets helps eliminate a problem that occurs with URLs, which often contain miscellaneous marks of punctuation, including hyphens and periods, so readers have trouble determining whether a particular punctuation mark is part of the URL. Look at this sentence:

- *Be sure to check out the information about this book and lots of our other fine publications at <www.-i-love-angle-brackets.net/-angle.brackets>.*

By putting the URL inside brackets this way, readers can tell that the closing period is the end of the sentence and isn't part of the URL. If you've ever typed a URL incorrectly, you'll know how frustrating it can be to try to find one little mistake. Using angle brackets can help eliminate that.

Good Grammar Tip

Some style guides will dictate that you put e-mail addresses in angle brackets, too.
E-mail me at <anglebracketsRfun@newyork.net>.

In the sample sentence at the start of this section, the brackets are enclosing information (*was very late*) that's essential to the meaning of the sentence. Insofar as brackets are needed at all, you can use them to enclose information that's nonessential.

Right: *"He [Justin] was very late to his own birthday party but didn't even apologize."*

Wrong: *"Marilyn loved Frank but . . . thought he was unreliable/irresponsible."*

Misuse of Ellipses and Slashes

Ellipsis points or marks (three spaced periods) let readers know that some material from a quotation has been omitted. Look at this sentence:

- *Marilyn loved Frank, but her parents, with whom she lived, thought he was unreliable.*

If you needed to quote that sentence but the part about living with her parents had no relevance to what you were saying, you could use ellipsis points in this way:

- *"Marilyn loved Frank, but her parents . . . thought he was unreliable."*

You should use ellipsis points only if the meaning of the sentence isn't changed by what you omit.

Suppose you have this sentence:

- *The policeman told Marilyn, "Frank has been involved in an accident and the other party is suspected of driving in a stolen car."*

You shouldn't use ellipsis marks to shorten it this way:

- *The policeman told Marilyn, "Frank has been involved in an accident and . . . is suspected of driving in a stolen car."*

In doing so you've twisted the meaning of the sentence as to point the finger of suspicion at poor Frank.

If the material you're omitting occurs at the end of a sentence, or if you omit the last part of a quoted sentence but what is left remains grammatically complete, use four ellipsis points, with the first one functioning as a period. Take this original passage:

- *"A number of new people have joined the after-school football club. The school administration has been extremely supportive. Parents are showing a lot of school spirit and have volunteered to buy the kids uniforms."*

You could use ellipsis marks in these ways:

- *"A number of new people have joined after-school football club. . . . Parents are showing a lot of school spirit and have volunteered to buy the kids uniforms."*

Another use for ellipsis marks comes if you're quoting someone and trying to show that there's a deliberate pause in what the person said. Read the following paragraph:

- *Jimmy thought to himself, "If I can just hold on to the ball long enough to get it over to Mike, I know he can get the shot off. . . . I have to pace myself. . . . Twenty-five seconds . . . fifteen seconds . . . eight seconds . . . Time for a pass."*

The ellipsis marks tell your readers that they're reading all of Jimmy's thoughts and that Jimmy wasn't interrupted by anything, he just didn't have any conscious thoughts in the intervening time indicated by the ellipsis marks.

From ellipses, let's turn to the often misused slash/virgule/solidus. What? You say you didn't know that a slash is also called a virgule and a solidus? Now, aren't you glad that you bought this book?

A virgule/slash/solidus is commonly used to mean *or*. Thus:

- *A slash/virgule/solidus = a slash or virgule or solidus*

- *You may bring your spouse/significant other to the picnic = You may bring your spouse or significant other to the picnic*

Notice that the two terms separated by the slash must be related to one another. You wouldn't say, for instance:

- *You may bring your spouse/potato salad to the picnic.*

If you were to say something like that, you'd probably get some pretty peculiar looks from your fellow picnickers.

In mathematics, the slash means *per*, as in this sentence:

- *There are 5,280 feet/mile.*

It's also used in fractions:

- *365/296 (meaning 365 divided by 296)*

In literature, the slash separates lines of poetry that are quoted inline style, as in this passage from Edgar Allan Poe's *The Raven*:

- *"Once upon a midnight dreary, while I pondered, weak and weary, / Over many a quaint and curious volume of forgotten lore—"*

Good Grammar Tip

In conjunction with modern efforts to be gender neutral, writers often use the combinations he/she, s/he, him/her, and his/hers. Too many of these combinations can get awkward, and, in fact, some style guides ban them altogether. To avoid them, rewrite the sentence, if possible.

Today the most common use of a slash is in URLs. If you've ever inadvertently omitted a slash when you're typing an address, you know that getting the site to open is impossible.

Right: *"Marilyn loved Frank but her parents . . . thought he was unreliable/irresponsible."*

[Part II]

Mixed-Up Words
(and How to Unmix Them)

Wrong: *On our walk in the woods we saw
a mommy deer and two baby deers.*

Problems with Plural Nouns

Let's say you're making a list of items from your home to take to a local charity. Are you donating two chairs or two chaires? three clocks or three clockes? five knives or five knifes? a picture of six deers or a picture of six deer? You get the picture; plurals in English are formed in any number of ways.

Good Grammar Tips

Often-confused Latin singulars and plurals include:

Singular	Plural
criterion	criteria
datum	data
erratum	errata
minutia	minutiae
phylum	phyla
septum	septa
stimulus	stimuli
syllabus	syllabuses/syllabi

- To form the plural of most English words that don't end in *-s*, *-z*, *-x*, *-sh*, *-ch*, or *-ss*, add *-s* at the end: desk = desks, book = books, cup = cups.
- To form the plural of most English words that end in *-s*, *-z*, *-x*, *-sh*, *-ch*, and *-ss*, add *-es* at the end: bus = buses, buzz = buzzes, box = boxes, dish = dishes, church = churches, kiss = kisses. Exceptions to this rule include *quizzes*, *frizzes*, and *whizzes*. (Note the doubled *-z*.)
- To form the plural of some English words that end in *-o*, add *-es* at the end: potato = potatoes, echo = echoes, hero = heroes.

- To make things interesting, other words that end in *-o* add only *-s* at the end: auto = autos, alto = altos, two = twos, zoo = zoos.
- And—just to keep you on your toes—some words ending in *-o* can form the plural in multiple ways: buffalo = buffalo/buffaloes/buffalos, cargo = cargoes/cargos, ghetto = ghettos/ghettoes

When in doubt about which form to use, consult your dictionary (check to see if your instructor or company prefers a particular dictionary) and use the plural form listed first.

- To form the plural of most English words that end in a consonant plus *-y*, change the *y* to *i* and add *-es*: lady = ladies, candy = candies, penny = pennies.
- To form the plural of most English words that end in a vowel plus *-y*, add *-s*: joy = joys, day = days, key = keys.
- To form the plural of most English words that end in *-f* or *-fe*, change the *f* to *v* and add *-es*: knife = knives, leaf = leaves, wife = wives.
  - Some exceptions to this rule (didn't you know there would be exceptions?) include *chef, cliff, belief, tariff, bailiff, roof,* and *chief.* All simply add *-s* to form their plural.
- Some words form their plurals in ways that defy categories: child = children, mouse = mice, foot = feet, person = people, tooth = teeth, ox = oxen.
- And—to confuse matters further—some words are the same in both singular and plural: deer, offspring, crossroads.

Good Grammar Tip

What's odd about the nouns: *ides, means, mathematics, outskirts, goods, economics, cattle, clothes, alms?*

They're among the nouns that don't have a singular form.

In the next section, you'll find spelling rules about prefixes and suffixes.

Many words that have come into English from other languages retain their original method of constructing plurals. Here are some of them:

Latin	
one alumnus	*two alumni*
one radius	*two radii*
Greek	
one analysis	*two analyses*
one diagnosis	*two diagnoses*

Right: *On our walk in the woods we saw a mommy deer and two baby deer.*

Wrong: *The picnicers brought their own carryer*
for their drinks and food.

Incorrect Suffixes and Prefixes

A number of the words we use today are shaped from prefixes, root words, and suffixes that originally came from many other languages, especially Latin, Greek, Old English, and French. By learning some of these, you can analyze unfamiliar words, break them down into their component parts, and then apply their meanings to help unlock their definitions.

Root words (base words) can add either prefixes or suffixes to create other words. Take, for instance, the root word *bene*, meaning *good*. If you add various prefixes (letters that come at the beginning of a word) and suffixes (letters that come at the end of a word) to *bene*, you can create other words such as *benefit, benevolent, benediction*, and *unbeneficial*. Each prefix and suffix has a meaning of its own; so by adding one or the other—or both—to root words, you form new words. You can see the root word *bene* in each of the new words, and each of the new words still retains a meaning having to do with *good*, but the prefix or suffix changes or expands on the meaning. (The prefix *un-*, for instance, means *not*. That gives a whole new meaning—an opposite meaning—to the word *unbeneficial*.)

In another example, look at the root word *chron*, which comes from Greek and means *time*. Adding the prefix *syn-* (meaning *together; with*) and the suffix *-ize* (meaning *to cause to be*) creates the modern word *synchronize*, which means *to set various timepieces at the same time*. Use a different suffix, *-ology*, meaning *the study of,* and you have *chronology*, which means *the study that deals with time divisions and assigns events to their proper dates.*

Interesting, too, is the way ancient word forms have been used to create words in modern times. Two thousand years ago, for instance, no one knew there would be a need for a word that meant *sending your voice far away*—but that's what the modern word *telephone* means. It's a combination of *tele*, meaning *distant or far away*, and *phon*, meaning *voice or sound.*

Here are some rules for spelling words to which prefixes or suffixes have been added:

- Words that end in *-x* don't change when a suffix is added to them:
  fax = faxing, hoax = hoaxed, mix = mixer.
- Words that end in *-c* don't change when a suffix is added to them if the letter before the *c* is *a, o, u,* or a consonant:
  talc = talcum, maniac = maniacal.
- Words that end in *-c* usually add *k* when a suffix is added to them if the letter before the *c* is *e* or *i* and the pronunciation of the *c* is hard:
  picnic = picnickers, colic = colicky, frolic = frolicking.
- Words that end in *-c* usually don't change when a suffix is added to them if the letter before the *c* is *e* or *i* and the pronunciation of the *c* is soft:
  critic = criticism, clinic = clinician, lyric = lyricist.
- Words that end in a single consonant immediately preceded by one or more unstressed vowels usually remain unchanged before any suffix:
  debit = debited, credit = creditor, felon = felony.
- Of course, you'll find exceptions, such as:
  program = programmed, format = formatting, crystal = crystallize.
- When a prefix is added to form a new word, the root word usually remains unchanged:
  spell = misspell, cast = recast, approve = disapprove.

In some cases, however, the new word is hyphenated. These exceptions include instances when the last letter of the prefix and the first letter of the word it's joining are the same vowel; when the prefix is being added to a proper noun; and when the new word formed by the prefix and the root must be distinguished from another word spelled in the same way but with a different meaning: *anti-institutional, mid-March, re-creation* (versus *recreation*).

- When adding a suffix to a word ending in *-y*, change the *y* to *i* when the *y* is preceded by a consonant:
  carry = carrier, irony = ironic, empty = emptied.

- This rule doesn't apply to words with an *-ing* ending:
  carry = carrying, empty = emptying.
- This rule also doesn't apply to words in which the *-y* is preceded by a vowel:
  delay = delayed, enjoy = enjoyable.
- Two or more words that join to form a compound word usually keep the original spelling of each word:
  cufflink, billfold, bookcase, football.
- If a word ends in *-ie*, change the *-ie* to *-y* before adding *-ing*:
  die = dying, lie = lying, tie = tying.
- When adding *-full* to the end of a word, change the ending to *-ful*:
  armful, grateful, careful.

Right: *The picnickers brought their own carrier*
for their drinks and food.

Wrong: *Bill was more in love with Jenna than I.*

Misuse of *Than* and *As*

A problem with pronouns sometimes arises in a sentence with words that are omitted following than *or* as.

Look at the following examples:

- *Jim said to Donna, "I always thought Billy liked you more than me."*

- *Jim said to Donna, "I always thought Billy liked you more than I."*

When the words that have been omitted after *than* are restored, the real meaning of the sentences becomes clear:

- *Jim said to Donna, "I always thought Billy liked you more than (he liked) me."*

- *Jim said to Donna, "I always thought Billy liked you more than I (liked you)."*

(Either way, Jim's in quite a snit, isn't he?) The same type of confusion can result when words following *as* have been omitted. For example, someone might say or write something along the lines of:

- *My husband finds physics as interesting as me.*

This implies that, to the husband, physics and his wife are of equal interest. Now, look at the correction:

- *My husband finds physics as interesting as I (do).*

This signifies that both spouses are equally interested in physics—which, one hopes, is the intended meaning here.

By adding the missing verb at the end of a sentence using *than* or *as* in this way, you'll be able to tell which pronoun to use.

Right: *Bill was more in love with Jenna than I was.*

> **Wrong:** *The guy who you telephoned at 2 A.M.*
> *is on the phone, and he sounds mad.*

Who versus *Whom*

For many people, deciding whether to use who *or* whom *may be the most difficult of all the problems with pronouns. Do you say, "The man who I called has already placed an order" or "The man whom I called has already placed an order"? How can you make up your mind between "The student who is early will get the best seat" and "The student whom is early will get the best seat"?*

If you have trouble deciding whether to use *who* or *whom* (or *whoever* or *whomever*), try the following method. It substitutes *he* and *him* for *who* and *whom* and provides a mnemonic for remembering when you should use which pronoun.

Good Grammar Tip

The use of *whom* is gradually decreasing in casual speaking, although many people are still careful about its use. Generally, its use—its correct use—is still important in writing.

First, remember to look only at the clause (a set of words with a subject and its verb) associated with *who* or *whom*. Some sentences have only one clause, and that makes finding the right word easy. Often, though, a sentence has more than one clause (an independent clause and one or more dependent clauses).

Next, scramble the words of the clause (if you have to) so that the words form a statement, not a question.

Now, substitute either *he* or *him* for *who* or *whom*. This will tell you whether to use *who* or *whom*. Use the mnemonic *he* = *who*, *hiM* = *whoM* (the final *m* helps you remember the association). If your sentence is about females only, pretend they're males for the sake of your mnemonic.

Be on the lookout for predicate nominatives. After you scramble the words, if you have a linking verb rather than an action verb, use *he* (*who*) instead of *him* (*whom*).

Ready to put all of this to a test? Try this sentence:

- *(Who, Whom) telephoned late last night?*

Since the sentence has only one clause, all you need to do is see if it's necessary to scramble the words to make a statement. In this sentence, no scrambling is necessary. You can substitute *he* and have a perfectly good sentence: *He telephoned late last night.* Since you substituted *he* instead of *him* (remember that *he* = *who*), you know to use *who* in the original question.

Good Grammar Tip

An independent clause is a set of words with a subject and its verb that expresses a complete thought; it could stand alone as a sentence. A dependent clause—while having a subject and verb—makes no sense by itself; it can't stand alone as a sentence.

Now, try this example:

- *(Who, Whom) were you telephoning late at night?*

This sentence also has only one clause that you have to deal with. Scramble the words to make a statement; then substitute *he* or *him*, and you have the statement "You were telephoning him late at night." Since you used *him* in the new sentence, you know to use *whom* in the original question.

Now for a trickier example:

- *Eugene worried about (who, whom) Ike would be teamed with in the competition.*

As you can tell, this sentence has two clauses (you could tell that, couldn't you?). Remember that you're *only* concerned with the clause that contains the *who/whom* question. In this case, take the words after *about*, scramble them to make a statement, substitute *he* or *him*, and you have "Eugene would be teamed with him in the competition." Since you used *him*, you would know that the original sentence would use *whom* (remember the mnemonic *him* = *whom*). So the original sentence would read this way:

- *Eugene worried about whom Ike would be teamed with in the competition.*

Here's another example that you have to stop and think about:

- *Was that (who, whom) you thought it was?*

When you look *only* at the clause the *who/whom* is concerned with and you substitute *he/him*, you have "it was he/him." A light bulb goes off in your head because you recognize that *was* is a linking verb. A linking verb requires the predicate nominative . . . which tells you to use *he*.

Right: *The guy whom you telephoned at 2 A.M. is on the phone, and he sounds mad.*

Wrong: *Far be it for me to suggest that this country's nucular policies are out of wack with the times.*

Misused Phrases

Misused phrases are very common. Don't feel as if you have to hang your head in shame if you see your own mistakes reported here; the point is to learn from them (and to promise yourself you'll never make them again).

Sometimes people hear certain nifty or impressive phrases and then later use those same phrases in their own writing or speech. Problems arise when they either misheard the phrase or remembered it incorrectly. What they end up writing or saying is close to the original, but it's not quite right.

The result is often a humorous take on the correct phrase (like a *doggie-dog world* instead of a *dog-eat-dog world*), and sometimes it's just plain puzzling (*beckon call* instead of *beck and call*).

The following are some of the more common mistakes of this variety, as reported by copyeditors and teachers. Have you made any of these mistakes? (Just nod silently. Now you'll know what to write next time.)

The Correct Phrase	What You'll Sometimes See or Hear
all it entails	*all it in tails*
all of a sudden	*all of the sudden*
beck and call	*beckon call*
bated breath	*baited breath*
begging the question	*bagging the question*
beside the point	*besides the point*
by accident	*on accident*
can't fathom it	*can't phantom it*
down the pike	*down the pipe*
dyed in the wool	*died in the wool*
en route to a party	*in route (or) in root to a party*

far be it from me	*far be it for me*
for all intents and purposes	*for all intensive purposes*
free rein	*free reign*
got my dander up	*got my dandruff up*
got his just deserts	*got his just desserts*
had the wherewithal	*had the where with all*
home in on	*hone in on*
I couldn't care less	*I could care less*
I hope to be at work	*hopefully, I'll be at work*
in his sights	*in his sites*
mind your p's and q's	*mind your peas and cues*
moot point	*mute point*
nip it in the bud	*nip it in the butt*
nuclear power	*nucular power*
one's surname	*one's sir name*
out of whack	*out of wack*
pored over a document	*poured over a document*
prostate cancer	*prostrate cancer*
recent poll	*recent pole*
shoo-in to win	*shoe-in to win*
supposedly	*supposably*
take it for granted	*take it for granite*
the die is cast	*the dye is cast*
toe the line	*towed the line*
tongue in cheek	*tongue and cheek*
up and at 'em	*up and adam*
whet my appetite	*wet my appetite*

Right: *Far be it from me to suggest that this country's nuclear policies are out of whack with the times.*

Wrong: *The policeman lay the picture of the hung criminal on the table.*

Incorrect Irregular Verbs

The good news is that most English verbs form their past and past participle by adding -d or -ed to the base form of the verb (the form you'd find listed first in the dictionary). These are called regular verbs.

Good Grammar Tip

Just to keep you on your toes, two verbs—*hang and lie*—may be regular or irregular, depending on their meaning in the sentence. If *hang* means *to use a noose*, it's a regular verb. If it means *to affix to a wall*, it's irregular. For example:

Prison officials discovered a picture the hanged man's mother had hung in his cell.

If *lie* means *to tell a falsehood*, it's a regular verb. If it means *to rest or recline*, it's irregular. Here's an example:

Dave lay on the cot and lied about his role in the murder.

The bad news is that English has a number of verb forms that aren't formed in that way; some people call them "those %*#@^ verbs," but usually they're called irregular verbs (clever, huh?). In Appendix B you'll find a list of often-used irregular English verbs.

Right: *The policeman laid the picture of the hanged criminal on the table.*

Wrong: *Helen picks up the letter that are lying on the table.*

Getting Verb-Subject Agreement Wrong

Do you ever notice some kind of incompatibility in your sentences? When you read your sentences, do you hear a jarring ring that tells you that something's wrong? The problem may be that you have disagreement between your subjects and verbs. To smooth out the situation, all you need to do is be sure that you follow the rule about subject-verb agreement: You must make verbs agree with their subjects in number and in person.

Okay, that's the rule, but what does it mean? The first part *(make the verb agree with its subject in number)* is just this simple: If you use a singular subject, you have to use a singular verb; if you use a plural subject, you have to use a plural verb. Nothing hard about that, is there?

Well, as you probably suspect, a number of situations can arise to make the rule tricky.

One problem comes with using the wrong word as your subject. To keep from making this mistake, remember this hint: Mentally disregard any **prepositional phrases** that come after the subject. Prepositional phrases will just distract you. Take a look at these sentences:

- *The tray of ice cubes (has, have) fallen on the kitchen floor.*

Since the subject of the sentence is *tray*, we can mentally cross out *of ice cubes* (which is a prepositional phrase):

- *The tray (has, have) fallen on the kitchen floor.*

Now, you're left with the subject of the sentence (*tray*). Of course, you would say,

- *The tray has fallen on the kitchen floor.*

Look at another example:

- *Katie and Matt, along with their dog Pretzel, (was, were) running through the yard when they upset an entire tray of drinks.*

Again, mentally cross off the prepositional phrase—no matter how long it is. We'll take poor little Pretzel out of things and get:

• *Katie and Matt (was, were) running through the yard when they upset an entire tray of drinks.*

You'd have no problem saying "Katie and Matt were running through the yard," so that lets you know the correct verb to use, and we can let them and Pretzel figure out how to explain the spilled drinks.

If an indefinite pronoun is the subject of your sentence, you have to look at the individual pronoun. Sometimes this is a snap, as with the plural pronouns that take a plural verb (*both, few, many, others, several*). Look at these sentences:

• *"Several scouts are (not is) in the stands at tonight's game," whispered the coach.*

• *"A few of us want [not wants] to go camping this weekend.*

Just as some plural indefinite pronouns are easy to spot, so are some singular indefinite pronouns (*another, anybody, anyone, anything, each, either, everybody, everyone, everything, much, neither, no one, nobody, nothing, one, other, somebody, someone, something*). The problem with indefinite pronouns is that a few of them are considered to be singular, even though they indicate a plural number (e.g., *each, everybody, everyone, everything*). For example:

• *Everybody is (not are) here, so we can start the trip.*

• *No one is (not are) going to complain if you pick up the tab for tonight's meal.*

Now comes a tricky rule: Five pronouns (*all, any, most, none,* and *some*) sometimes take a singular verb and sometimes take a plural verb. How do you know which one to use? This is the time—the only time—you break the rule about disregarding the prepositional phrases. Take a look at these sentences:

• *"Some of the money is (not are) missing!" cried the teller.*

• *"Some of the people in the bank are (not is) the suspects," replied the policeman.*

- *Most of my coworkers were (not* was*) cleared of any suspicion*

- *Most of my jewelry is (not* are*) still missing.*

In each case, you have to look at the object of the preposition (*money, people, coworkers, jewelry*) to decide whether to use a singular or plural verb.

Here are some more oddities of English grammar (as if you haven't seen enough of them already):

The phrase *the only one of those* uses a singular verb; however, the phrase *one of those* uses a plural verb. (Is your head spinning?) Maybe these examples will help:

- *The only one of those people I don't suspect is (not* are*) Vicki Brand.*

- *Vicki Brand is one of those people who always seem (not* seems*) completely honest.*

If you have a sentence with *every* or *many a* before a word or group of words, use a singular verb. For example:

- *Many a good man is (not* are*) trying to please his wife.*

- *Every wife tries (not* try*) to help her husband understand.*

When the phrase *the number* is part of the subject of a sentence, it takes a singular verb. When the phrase *a number* is part of the subject, it takes a plural verb. Look at these sentences:

- *The number of people who came to the concert is [not* are*] disappointing.*

- *A number of people are (not* is*) at home watching the finals of the basketball tournament.*

When the phrase *more than one* is part of the subject, it takes a singular verb:

- *More than one person is (not* are*) upset about the decline of culture in this country.*

Another time that subjects may be singular or plural is with collective nouns. Collective nouns (*cast, fleet,* or *gang*) name groups. Use a singular verb if you mean that the individual members of the group act or think together (they act as one unit). Use a plural verb if you mean that the individual members of the group act or think separately (they have different opinions or actions). For example:

- *The couple is renewing its donation of $50,000 for scholarships.*

(The two people were donating as a unit.)

- *The couple were praised for their public spirit.*

(The two were praised separately.)

Still another problem with singular and plural verbs comes with expressions of amount. When the particular measurement or quantity (e.g., of time, money, weight, volume, food, or fractions) is considered as one unit or group, then use a singular verb:

- *Ten dollars to see this movie is (not* are*) highway robbery!*

- *"Five hours is (not* are*) too long to sit in a theater watching a play,"* complained the angry patron of the arts.

- *I would estimate that two-thirds of the audience has (not* have*) walked out.*

Some nouns look plural but actually name one person, place, or thing, and so they're singular:

- *The United States is (not* are*) defending its title against the United Kingdom.*

(Although fifty states are in the United States, it's one country; therefore, you use a singular verb.)

- If I Was You . . . *is (not* are*) the best grammar book I've ever read!*

(Even though four words are in the title, *If I Was You . . .* is one book; use a singular verb.)

• *Because I find the subject fascinating, I think it's odd that economics is (not are) called the dismal science.*

(*Economics* looks as if it's a plural word, but since it's one subject it needs a singular verb.)

Good Grammar Tip

Most *-ics* words (e.g., *mechanics, acrobatics,* and *electronics*) are singular.

Here's another special situation: When you use the words *pants, trousers, shears, spectacles, glasses, tongs,* and *scissors* alone, you use a plural verb:

• *These pants are (not are) too tight since I returned from the cruise.*

• *Do (not Does) these trousers come in another color?*

But put the words *a pair of* in front of *pants, trousers, shears, spectacles, glasses, tongs,* or *scissors,* and then you need a singular verb:

• *This pair of pants is (not are) too tight since I returned home from the cruise.*

• *Does (not Do) this pair of trousers come in another color?*

If you think about it, the logic behind the usage is strange since *pair* means *two,* and *two* denotes a plural. Oh, well . . .

But what about **compound subjects**? Well, the first rule in this part is easy. Compound subjects (subjects joined by *and*) take a plural verb:

• *Mike and Lynn are (not is) here.*

• *Mr. and Mrs. Cox are (not is) out for a romantic dinner together.*

Here's an exception: If you have two or more subjects joined by *and*— and the subjects are thought of as one unit—then use a singular verb.

• *Is spaghetti and meatballs the special at Rookie's Restaurant today?*

The second rule is *almost* as easy. Singular subjects joined by *or* or *nor* take a singular verb:

- *The butcher, the baker, or the candlestick maker is (not* are*) coming to tomorrow's career fair.*

Rule number three is along the same lines as rule number two (and it's also *almost* as easy as the first rule). Plural subjects joined by *or* or *nor* take a plural verb:

- *The Paynes or the Meaghers are (not* is*) visiting tonight.*

- *The children or the pigs are (not* is*) making too much noise tonight.*

Did you notice the word *almost* in the second and third rules? The first rule was easy; all you had to do was look at subjects joined by *and*; then use a plural verb. The second and third rules require just a little more thought because you have to be sure that the subjects joined by *or* or *nor* are either *all* singular or *all* plural:

- If all the subjects are singular, use a singular verb.
- If all the subjects are plural, use a plural verb.

That covers all the examples in which the subjects are the same, but what if you have one singular subject and one plural subject joined by *or* or *nor*? Do you use a singular or plural verb? Simple: You go by the subject that's closer to the verb. So you would write:

- *My cat or my three dogs are (not* is, *since* dogs *is plural and is closer to the verb) coming with me.*

Or, if you inverted the subjects, you'd write:

- *My three dogs or my cat is (not* are, *since* cat *is singular and is closer to the verb) making me itch.*

Sometimes writers and speakers have a hard time with sentences that begin with *here* or *there*. Writing either

- *Here's the money for taking care of my cat.*

or

- *There's a little extra to cover the damage to your furniture.*

Both of these are fine because if you changed the contractions into the two words each represents, you'd have "Here is the money for taking care of my cat" and "There is a little extra to cover the damage to your furniture."

No problem, huh? I mean, beyond the ruined furniture. Now look at these sentences:

- *Here's the new chairs Marsha and Morris said they'd bring.*

- *There's lots of sandwiches left, so help yourself.*

In these examples if you change those contractions, you have "Here is the chairs Marsha and Morris said they'd bring" and "There is lots of sandwiches left, so help yourself." Obviously, you'd never say, "Here is the chairs" or "There is lots of sandwiches" (you wouldn't, would you?), so the verb form is wrong. Since each of those subjects is plural, you need the plural verb (*are*).

So the rule is this: If you begin a sentence with *here* or *there* and you have a plural subject, be sure to use a plural verb (usually the verb *are*).

Right: *Helen picks up the letter that is lying on the table.*

Wrong: *The flag blowing in the wind seemed hope to us all.*

Misusing Linking Verbs

The definition for be verbs *says they "usually" are forms of* be. *Just to complicate the situation, the words in the following list can sometimes be used as linking verbs (or you may know them as copulative verbs, depending on when you went to school).*

The following verbs can be either linking verbs or action verbs:

appear	*become*	*feel*
grow	*look*	*prove*
remain	*seem*	*smell*
sound	*stay*	*taste*

So when are these twelve verbs action verbs, and when are they linking verbs? Use this test: If you can substitute a form of *be* (*am, is, was,* and so on) and the sentence still makes sense, by golly, you've got yourself a linking verb. Look at these examples:

- *The soup tasted too spicy for me.*

Substitute *was* or *is* for *tasted* and you have this sentence:

- *The soup was (is) too spicy for me.*

It makes perfect sense. You have a linking verb. Now look at this one:

- *I tasted the spicy soup.*

Substitute *was* or *is* for *tasted* and you have this sentence:

- *I was (is) the spicy soup.*

That doesn't make much sense, does it? Since the substitution of a *be* verb doesn't make sense, you don't have a linking verb. You can try the same trick by substituting a form of *seem*:

- *The soup tasted too spicy for me.*

Substitute *seemed* and you have the following:

- *The soup seemed too spicy for me.*

The sentence makes sense, so *tasted* is a linking verb.
If you try the same trick with this sentence:

- *I tasted the spicy soup.*

You get:

- *I seemed the spicy soup.*

That doesn't make sense, so *tasted* isn't a linking verb in this sentence.

Another type of verb that may appear in a sentence is a helping (auxiliary) verb. This can join the main verb (becoming the helper of the main verb) to express the tense, mood, and voice of the verb. Common helping verbs are *be, do, have, can, may,* and so on. (The first two sentences of this paragraph have helping verbs: *may* and *can*.)

Other kinds of complements, called subject complements, are used only with linking verbs. (Linking verbs, you'll remember, are all forms of *be* and, in certain situations, *appear, become, feel, grow, look, remain, smell, sound, stay,* and *taste*.) Subject complements do just what their name implies—they complete (give you more information about) the subject. Predicate adjectives and predicate nominatives are the two types of subject complements.

Now let's consider predicate adjectives. A predicate adjective is an adjective that comes after a linking verb and describes the subject of the sentence. To find a predicate adjective, apply this formula:

- First, make sure the sentence has a linking verb.
- Second, find the subject of the sentence.
- Third, say the subject, say the linking verb, and then ask *what?* If a word answers the question *what?* and is an adjective, then you have a predicate adjective.

Here's an example of a predicate adjective:

- *Members of the Outlook Book Club are all intelligent.*

Apply the formula to the preceding sentence: (1) you know that *are* is a linking verb; (2) you find *members* as the subject of the sentence; (3) you say *members are what?* Since *intelligent* answers that question, and *intelligent* is an adjective (it describes the noun *members*), then you know that *intelligent* is a predicate adjective.

The other type of subject complement is the predicate nominative (predicate noun). It also comes after a linking verb and gives you more information about the subject. A predicate nominative, however, must be a noun or pronoun. Here's a formula for finding a predicate nominative:

- First, make sure the sentence has a linking verb.
- Second, find the subject of the sentence.
- Third, say the subject, say the linking verb, and then ask *who?* or *what?* If a word answers the question *who?* or *what?* and is a noun or pronoun, you have a predicate nominative.

Good Grammar Tip

Just like subjects and predicates, any kind of complement may be compound.

I played basketball and football in high school.

(compound direct objects)

Lynne and Dick bought their dogs Bow and Wow new engraved collars.

(compound object complements)

Tony brought Margaret and Todd a hamburger for lunch.

(compound indirect objects)

Andrew and Richard felt elated and nervous about playing in their first game.

(compound predicate adjectives)

Lucy is my aunt and my friend.

(compound predicate nominatives)

Look at this sentence:

- *That man over there is DeShawn.*

Apply the formula to the previous sentence: (1) you know that *is* is a linking verb; (2) you find *man* as the subject of the sentence; (3) you say *man is who?* Since *DeShawn* answers that question, and *DeShawn* is a noun (it names a person), then you know that *DeShawn* is a predicate nominative.

Right: *The flag blowing in the wind seemed hopeful to us all.*

Wrong: *Yesterday I ride into town to get news from the police.*

Getting the Wrong Verb Tense

English verbs are divided into three main tenses, all of which relate to time: present, past, and future. Each main tense is also subdivided into other categories: simple tense, progressive tense, perfect tense, and perfect progressive tense. These subcategories differentiate when a particular action has been done (or is being done or will be done).

Clear as mud? Take a look at this chart:

	Simple*	Progressive**	Perfect***	Perfect Progressive****
Present	hide	am/is/are hiding	have/has hidden	have/has been hiding
Past	hid	was/were hiding	had hidden	had been hiding
Future	will/shall hide	will be hiding	will have hidden	will have been hiding

*Indicates action that is usual or is repeated.
**Indicates action that is ongoing.
***Indicates action that is completed.
****Indicates ongoing action that will be completed at some definite time.

Each of these tenses signals the time something is done, will be done, or has been done relative to when it's being written or spoken about. You still don't quite get the whole thing? Don't worry; all will be cleared up in the next few pages, starting with explanations for each of the tenses. To lighten the mood, why don't we start with a little joke:

Professor Reynolds says to her student, "Conjugate the verb to walk *in the simple present tense."*

The student says, "I walk. You walk. He—"

Interrupting, Professor Reynolds says, "More quickly, please."

The student replies, "I run. You run . . ."

The **simple present tense** tells an action that is usual or repeated:

• *I hide from the stalker.*

Looked at in a different way, the simple present tense relates actions that happen often or that state a fact or opinion.

To make sure they're using the correct verb form for the present tense, some writers find it helpful to begin the example sentence with the word *today*:

• *Today I hide from the stalker.*

The **simple past tense** tells an action that both began and ended in the past:

• *I hid from the stalker.*

To make sure they're using the correct verb form for the past tense, some writers find it helpful to mentally begin the example sentence with the word *yesterday*:

• *Yesterday I hid from the stalker.*

The **simple future tense** tells an upcoming action that will occur:

• *I will hide from the stalker.*

To make sure they're using the correct verb form for the future tense, some writers find it helpful to mentally begin the example sentence with the word *tomorrow*:

• *Tomorrow I will hide from the stalker.*

That's simple enough, isn't it? It's the simple present tense. After this, though, the explanations of the other tenses get a little tricky—but you're up to the challenge, aren't you?

Use the **present progressive tense** to show an action that's in progress at the time the statement is written:

• *I am hiding from the stalker today.*

Present progressive verbs are always formed by using *am*, *is*, or *are* and adding *-ing* to the verb.

Use the **past progressive tense** to show an action that was going on at some particular time in the past:

- *I was hiding from the stalker yesterday.*

Past progressive verbs are always formed by using *was* or *were* and adding *-ing* to the verb.

Use the **future progressive tense** to show an action that's continuous and that will occur in the future:

- *I will be hiding from the stalker tomorrow.*

Future progressive verbs are always formed by using *will be* or *shall be* and adding *-ing* to the verb.

Use the **present perfect tense** to convey action that happened sometime in the past or that started in the past but is ongoing in the present:

- *I have hidden from the stalker for more than five years.*

Present perfect verbs are always formed by using *has* or *have* and the past participle form of the verb.

Use the **past perfect tense** to indicate past action that occurred prior to another past action:

- *I had hidden from the stalker for more than five years before I entered the Witness Protection Program.*

Past perfect verbs are always formed by using *had* and the past participle form of the verb.

Use the **future perfect tense** to illustrate future action that will occur before some other action:

- *I will have hidden from the stalker for more than five years before entering the Witness Protection Program.*

Future perfect verbs are always formed by using *will have* and the past participle form of the verb.

Use the **present perfect progressive** to illustrate an action repeated over a period of time in the past, continuing in the present, and possibly carrying on in the future:

- *For the past five years, I have been hiding from the stalker.*

Present perfect progressive verbs are always formed by using *has been* or *have been* and the past participle form of the verb.

Use the **past perfect progressive** to illustrate a past continuous action that was completed before some other past action:

- *Before I entered the Witness Protection Program, I had been hiding from the stalker for more than five years.*

Past perfect progressive verbs are always formed by using *had been* and adding *-ing* to the verb.

Use the **future perfect progressive** to illustrate a future continuous action that will be completed before some future time:

- *Next month I will have been hiding from the stalker for more than five years.*

Future perfect progressive verbs are always formed by using *will have been* and adding *-ing* to the verb.

Right: *Yesterday I rode into town to get news from the police.*

Wrong: *I wouldn't wear that outfit if I was you.*

Incorrect Mood

In addition to tenses, English verbs are divided into moods, which show the writer's attitude toward what he or she is saying. The first two moods, indicative and imperative, aren't confusing at all, and, fortunately, they're used far more frequently than the third mood, subjunctive.

Good Grammar Tip

Some grammarians add a fourth category of mood—interrogative—but most include interrogative sentences (you do remember that interrogative sentences ask a question, don't you?) in the indicative group.

Almost all verbs are used in the indicative mood, which means that the verb in the sentence states a fact or an actuality. All of these sentences are in the indicative mood:

• *I'll be seeing you later on tonight. Wear whatever you want. You look nice in anything. We're all casual dressers, so don't worry about your attire.*

Verbs used in the imperative mood are in sentences that make requests or give a command. All of these sentences are in the imperative mood:

• *Please give me the phone.*

• *Give it to me right now!*

• *Give it to me—or else!*

The subjunctive mood is the one that speakers and writers sometimes have problems with. Fortunately, it's used with only two verbs (*be* and *were*), and in modern English, it's used in only two kinds of sentences:

1. Statements that are contrary to fact (providing they begin with *if* or *unless*), improbable, or doubtful
2. Statements that express a wish, a request or recommendation, an urgent appeal, or a demand

The following are verb forms used in the subjunctive mood:

Present Subjunctive	
Singular	*Plural*
(if) I be	(if) we be
(if) you be	(if) you be
(if) he/she/it be	(if) they be
Past Subjunctive	
Singular	*Plural*
(if) I were	(if) we were
(if) you were	(if) you were
(if) he/she/it were	(if) they were

Here are several examples:

• *Mary Alice moved that the minutes be (not* are*) accepted.*

This statement expresses a request.

• *If I were (not* was*) a millionaire, I would never have to think about saving money.*

I'm not a millionaire, so the idea that I am is contrary to fact.

• *If Breck were (not* was*) here, he'd perform his magic tricks.*

Breck isn't here, so the statement is contrary to fact.

Good Grammar Tip

Some authorities hold that if the context is something that *could* be possible, it's okay to use was instead of were. Others, however, are more rigid on the question.

This is a wish or demand.

- *It's important that everybody be (not is) at the meeting.*

This is a wish or request—a strong request, at that.

Right: *I wouldn't wear that outfit if I were you.*

Wrong: *The difficulties of the city are being addressed by the council.*

Active versus Passive Voice

Except for certain scientific material, you should write using the active voice whenever possible. If you have a number of sentences that contain be verbs (is, are, was, were, and so on), change the structure of your sentence. For instance, you could change:

- *The downtown area is enhanced by the new streetlights. (passive voice)*

to

- *The new streetlights enhance the downtown area. (active voice)*

Along the same lines, look for sentences that begin with expletives like *it*, *this*, or *there*; these sentences often become more forceful when you reword them. If you've written, for instance:

- *There are six changes that should be made in the method of administration of the school system.*

you can make the sentence stronger by changing it to:

- *Officials should make six changes in the administrative method of the school system.*

This uses the active voice to make the point that the officials should get on the ball and do their jobs.

Right: *The council is addressing the city's difficulties.*

Wrong: *That was the most scary movie I've seen since I watched* The Blair Witch Project.

Wrong Adverbial Comparisons

Sometimes you need to show how something compares with or measures up to something else. Say, for example, you and your family enjoy watching horror movies. You may want to report about a new scary movie you've seen and decide whether it's scarier than another one you've all recently watched together or perhaps even the scariest movie you've ever seen (in which case, you might have some serious nightmares!). A scary movie can become a scarier movie if it's compared to another one, or it can become the scariest movie if it's compared to several others. You get the picture?

In writing comparisons, you use one of three different forms (called degrees) of adjectives and adverbs:

The positive degree simply makes a statement about a person, place, or thing.

The comparative degree compares two (but only two) people, places, or things.

The superlative degree compares more than two people, places, or things.

Positive	Comparative	Superlative
pink	pinker	pinkest
dirty	dirtier	dirtiest
happy	happier	happiest
tall	taller	tallest

Here are a couple of rules to help you in forming the comparative and superlative:

- **Rule #1.** One-syllable adjectives and adverbs usually form their comparative form by adding *-er* and their superlative form by adding *-est* (see the examples *tall* and *pink* in the table).

- **Rule #2.** Adjectives of more than two syllables and adverbs ending in *-ly* usually form comparative forms by using *more* (or *less*) and superlative forms by using *most* (or *least*).

Positive	Comparative	Superlative
awkwardly	more awkwardly	most awkwardly
comfortable	more comfortable	most comfortable
qualified	less qualified	least qualified

- **Rule #3.** Confusion sometimes crops up in forming comparisons of words of two syllables only. Here's the rub: Sometimes two-syllable words use the *-er, est* forms, and sometimes they use the *more, most* (or *less, least*) forms. You knew there had to be some complications in there somewhere, didn't you?

Positive	Comparative	Superlative
sleepy	sleepier	sleepiest
tiring	more tiring	most tiring

So how do you know whether to use the *-er, est* form or the *more, most* form? You have to use a dictionary (a large dictionary, not a paperback one) if you're not sure. If no comparative or superlative forms are listed in the dictionary, use the *more, most* form.

Did you happen to notice the word *usually* in the first two rules? It's there because English has some exceptions to the rules. The good news is that the exceptions are few. Among them are:

Positive	Comparative	Superlative
bad	worse	worst
far	farther/further	farthest/furthest
good	better	best
well	better	best
ill	worse	worst

Positive	Comparative	Superlative
little	littler/less/lesser	littlest/least
many	more	most
much	more	most
old (persons)	elder	eldest
old (things)	older	oldest

Good Grammar Tip

Remember that some adjectives can't be compared. Words like *round*, *unique*, *favorite*, and *true* are already absolutes (for example, something can't be rounder than something else).

Before we get to the use of double negatives—one of the most noticeable blunders that can be made in the English language (and which you can probably spot a mile away)—let's first touch on a couple of other errors to avoid with comparisons.

One common mistake in both writing and speaking is to use the superlative form when the comparative should be used. If you're comparing two persons, places, or things, you use only the comparative form (not the superlative). Look at these sentences:

• *Between* Night of the Living Dead *and* 30 Days of Night, Living Dead *is the scariest.*

• *There are two Blair Witch movies:* The Blair Witch Project *is the oldest, and* Book of Shadows: Blair Witch 2 *is the newest.*

In both of those sentences, the comparison is between only two (*two movies*), so the sentences should be written with the comparative form (*scarier, older, newer*) instead of the superlative.

Another frequent mistake in comparisons is in going overboard—using both the *-er* and *more* or *-est* and *most* forms with the same noun, as in *the most tallest statue* or *a more happier child*. Remember that one form is the limit (and, of course, it has to be the correct form). In the examples, *most* and *more* need to be eliminated.

Sometimes comparisons can be ambiguous. Because some comparisons can be interpreted more than one way, be sure you include all the words necessary to give the meaning you intend.

Read this sentence:

• *In his skill at horror film direction, Roger Corman could beat John Carpenter more often than Wes Craven.*

Constructed that way, readers don't know if the meaning is the following:

• *In his skill at horror film direction, Roger Corman could beat John Carpenter more often than Wes Craven could.*

or

• *In his skill at horror film direction, Roger Corman could beat John Carpenter more often than he could beat Wes Craven.*

Depending on the meaning, either of these two sentences would be preferable to the first one.

Right: *That was the scariest movie I've seen since I watched* The Blair Witch Project.

[Part III]

Complicated Parts of Speech (and How to Untangle Them)

Wrong: *When our neighbors are out of town, we get the mail for her.*

Problems with Pronoun-Antecedent Agreement

Pronouns must agree in number with the words to which they refer (their antecedents). Read these sentences:

- *After I saw who wrote the letters, I tossed it into the wastebasket.*

- *After I saw who wrote the letters, I tossed them into the wastebasket.*

The first sentence doesn't make sense because *it* is the wrong pronoun. The noun that *it* refers to is *letters*, and *letters* is a plural noun. The pronoun used to replace *it* should also be plural. In the second sentence, *it* has been replaced by *them*, which is plural. That's why the second sentence makes sense.

Put another way, the rule is this: If a pronoun is plural, the word it refers to (also known as its antecedent) must be plural; if a pronoun is singular, the word it refers to must be singular.

So what's the problem? No one would write a sentence like the first example, right? But complications do arise where some of the indefinite pronouns are concerned.

Indefinite pronouns include the following:		
all	everyone	none
another	everything	nothing
any	few	one
anybody	little	other
anyone	many	others
anything	most	several
both	much	some
each	neither	somebody
either	no one	someone
everybody	nobody	something

Anyone, anybody, anything, each, either, everybody, everyone, everything, neither, nobody, none, no one, one, somebody, something, and *someone* are all considered to be singular words, so they all require a singular pronoun. But, if you think about it, the word *each* implies more than one. If each person is doing something, that means more than one, right? The same can be said for *everybody, everything,* and *everyone.* This doesn't matter; all four words are considered singular. So you should write:

- *Everybody is seated, and each is waiting for the plane to take off.*

- *Each of the dogs needs its carrier before it can be taken onto the plane.*

- *Everyone must bring a list of her prenatal vitamins. (Using only* her *in this sentence is perfectly fine since, presumably, no men would be taking prenatal vitamins.)*

A common tendency in everyday speech is to use *they* or *their* in place of some singular pronouns. In the first example, you might hear the sentence spoken this way:

- *Everybody is seated, and they are waiting for the plane to take off.*

This usage is called the "singular they" because *they* refers to an antecedent that's singular.

Even though using the "singular they" is becoming more commonplace, its usage is still frowned on in many circles. However, this may be one of the rules of grammar that eventually changes. The advocates of the "singular they" point out that using it helps prevent an overuse of *his or her* or *he or she.*

Now it's time to break a rule. Remember the one that says to disregard any prepositional phrase when you're looking for the subject of a sentence? Well, this rule has a few exceptions. Take a look at these two sentences:

- *All of the money is missing from the safe.*

- *All of the cookies are missing from the jar.*

In both sentences, the subject is *all.* But the first sentence has a singular verb and the second sentence has a plural verb—and both are correct.

With five pronouns (*all*, *any*, *most*, *none*, and *some*), the "disregard the prepositional phrase" rule is canceled out. For those five pronouns, look at the object of the preposition to determine which verb to use.

Good Grammar Tip

When you have compound antecedents that are joined by *or* or *nor* (or *either . . . or, neither . . . nor*), make the pronoun agree with the one that's closer to the verb. Here's an example:

Either the lion or the monkeys have already gotten their food.

Since *monkeys* is plural and it comes nearer the pronoun, use the plural pronoun *their*.

Either the monkeys or the lion has already gotten its food.

Since *lion* is singular and it comes nearer the pronoun, use the singular pronoun *its*.

So, do you think you can pinpoint the mistake in the following paragraph? Pronouns and their antecedents should agree in number.

• *When I came down to breakfast, everybody in the family was eating, but nobody offered me even a piece of toast. At work, everyone was busy doing their different projects; they didn't even stop to look up when I came in.*

By changing the incorrect pronouns, you should have:

• *When I came down to breakfast, everybody in the family was eating, but nobody offered me even a piece of toast. At work, everyone was busy doing his or her different projects; they didn't even stop to look up when I came in.*

You can see, though, that there's a definite problem with that rewriting. While it may be grammatically correct, it sure doesn't read well. Contrary to rules of thirty or more years ago, using *his or her* rather than just *his* is now considered correct. But as you can see in the corrected paragraph, this can make for some rather awkward writing.

So what can you do to prevent this awkwardness? Rewriting the sentences to use plural nouns and pronouns instead of singular ones is far better. The paragraph could be rewritten this way:

• *When I came down to breakfast, all of my family were already eating, but nobody offered me even a piece of toast. At work, all of my associates were already busy doing their different projects; they didn't even stop to look up when I came in.*

Much better, isn't it?

Right: *When our neighbor is out of town, we get the mail for her.*

> **Wrong:** *After putting the package in the car,*
> *Marilyn asked Frank to retrieve it.*

Poor Pronoun References

One of the most common writing problems occurs in sentences that have unclear antecedents. In the preceding sentence, is Marilyn asking Frank to retrieve the package or the car?

As you recall, pronouns are words that take the place of nouns; antecedents are the nouns that the pronouns refer to. For example:

• *Chelsea called to say she and Anthony would be glad to help Marilyn decorate for the party.*

In this sentence, the pronoun *she* refers to *Chelsea*; therefore, *Chelsea* is the antecedent of *she*. Now, look at this example:

• *Frank's skills were more muscular and they didn't extend to the fine arts.*

The pronoun *they* refers to *skills*; *skills* is the antecedent of *they*.

In these examples, the antecedents are used correctly. They clearly refer to specific nouns (their antecedents). But take a look at this sentence:

• *Anthony invited Frank to play pool because he enjoyed games of skill.*

Well, now. Just whom does the word *he* in the second part of the sentence refer to—Anthony or Frank? The antecedent of *he* isn't clear.

To make the sentence read clearly, it should be reworded:

• *Because Frank enjoyed games of skill, Anthony invited him to play pool.*

or

• *Anthony, who enjoyed games of skill, invited Frank to play pool.*

Now look at these sentences:

• *Pattye called Linda to report the unexpected news that she was bringing her ex-husband to the party.*

- *When Pattye told Claudia and Lorraine the news, she said that they should be happy for her.*

Are you confused? Whose ex-husband was coming—Pattye's or Linda's? Who said her friends should be happy for her—Pattye or Claudia or Lorraine? Who was to be included in the celebration—Pattye, Linda, Claudia, and Lorraine? For whom should they have been happy? The way the two sentences are now worded, readers aren't sure.

You can correct the first sentence in several ways, depending on whom you're referring to by the words *she* and *they*. Suppose Pattye is the one bringing the former spouse. One way to recast the sentence to express that meaning is this way:

- *Pattye, who was bringing her ex-husband to the party, called her friend Linda.*

Now there's no doubt about who's bringing this guy. If Linda's ex was involved, then the sentence could be reworded this way:

- *Linda called Pattye to report the unexpected news that Linda was bringing her ex-husband to the party.*

In the second sentence, who's going to celebrate? To make the meaning clearer, that sentence could be reworded this way:

- *Pattye told Claudia and Lorraine the news, and she also said that they all should celebrate.*

Now it's clear who announced the celebration and who was to be included in it.

Sometimes a pronoun has no reference at all. Read this sentence:

- *Cathy Blue was afraid he wouldn't remember to pick up the refreshments for the party.*

Just who is *he*? Unless the man has been identified in an earlier sentence, readers are left out in the cold about his identity.

Remember that an antecedent has to refer to a specific person, place, or thing. Look at this sentence:

- *The young man was elated, but he kept it hidden.*

What did the young man keep hidden? Was *it* supposed to refer to the fact that he felt elated? In that case, the sentence would read:

- *The young man was elated, but he kept elated hidden.*

Doesn't make sense, does it? The word *elated* can't be the antecedent of *it* because *elated* isn't a person, place, or thing. The sentence needs to be reworded something like this:

- *The young man was elated with his date, but he kept his feeling hidden.*

Along the same lines, sometimes a sentence has a noun that the pronoun refers to, but it's not the right noun; the correct reference is missing from the sentence. Read this sentence:

- *After a successful fishing trip with his brothers, Joe let them all go.*

The way the sentence is worded, Joe let his brothers go. That's what *them* refers to in this sentence. But surely that's not what happened! What the writer means is that Joe let all the fish go. The sentence should be rewritten like this:

- *After a successful fishing trip with his brothers, Joe let all their catch go.*

Good Grammar Tip

When you're referring to people, use *who, whom,* or *whose,* not *which* or *that.* Here's an incorrect sentence:

I'm indebted to the people that helped me during the flood.

Here's the sentence in the correct way:

I'm indebted to the people who helped me during the flood.

Here's another example of a pronoun that doesn't refer to the right antecedent:

• *The new tax forms arrived today. They want me to fill out every line on the last three pages.*

The tax forms want you to do the filling out? That's silly! What the writer meant was that the Internal Revenue Service, or an accounting firm, or the office personnel at work—someone the writer had failed to name—wants the tax forms filled out. The sentence needs to be reworded to make it clear who *they* are:

• *The new tax forms arrived today. Our accountant wants me to fill out every line on the last three pages.*

Be careful not to use *they* when you refer to unnamed persons; said another way, *they* must refer to people you specify. The same holds true for any pronoun, but *they, he, she,* and *it* are the ones most commonly misused in this way. If you think you may have an unclear reference, one way to test the sentence is to do this:

1. Find the pronoun.
2. Replace the pronoun with its antecedent—the noun it refers to (remember, the noun must be the exact word).
3. If the sentence doesn't make sense, reword it.

Right: *Marilyn asked Frank to retrieve the package, which she had put in the car.*

Wrong: *After I'm done filling out the form, we may be required to bring it to the office, where we'll have to submit it to the secretary.*

Misuse of Person

Often you may have instructions that call for your material (e.g., a paper, a resume, a memo) to be written in a particular person—first person, second person, or third person. That's fine, but what does it mean?

Both pronouns and points of view are expressed in first person, second person, and third person. You remember that first-person pronouns include *I, me, my, mine, we, our,* and *us* and the first-person point of view expresses the personal point of view of the speaker or author (*I will bring the book*). Second-person pronouns include *you, your,* and *yours,* and material expressed in the second-person point of view directly addresses the listener or reader (*You will bring the book*). Third-person pronouns include *he, she, him, her, his, hers, they, them, their,* and *theirs.* In the third-person point of view material is expressed from the point of view of a detached writer or other characters (*They will bring the book*).

Most instructors insist that academic writing be in the third person, although some now allow for first or second person, depending on the subject matter. If you're writing for classes, check with the instructors to determine if they have a requirement about using first, second, or third person. If you're writing for a company, check to see if particular guidelines are in place about which person you should use. (If you're still in doubt, use third person.)

One of the most common problems in writing comes with a shift in person, as illustrated by the sentence at the beginning of this section. The writer begins in first person singular and then—without reason—shifts to first person plural. Here's another example of the problem:

• *Even in a casual atmosphere, I can be embarrassed by someone else, and this causes you to become tense. For instance, somebody you don't know can embarrass you at a party or in a class. It's so simple for a stranger to embarrass you.*

What's wrong with that paragraph? The writer begins in the first person (telling about himself or herself by using the pronoun *I*) and then shifts to second person. The constant use of *you* sounds as if the writer is preaching directly to readers. That writer doesn't know the readers and doesn't know if he or she can be easily embarrassed by others, and so on. Except for the beginning sentence, the entire paragraph should be rewritten and put into first person. Here is one way of doing that:

• *Even in a casual atmosphere, I can be embarrassed by someone else, and this causes me to become tense. For instance, somebody I don't know can embarrass me at a party or in a class. It's so simple for a stranger to embarrass me.*

Repeat three times: Consistency is the key. Consistency is the key. Consistency is the key. If you begin in third person (which is the most common way of writing), stay in third person. If you begin in first person (the second most common way of writing), stay in first person. If you begin in second person, stay in second person. Consistency is the key.

(You did notice that the preceding paragraph is written in second person, didn't you? Actually, the first sentences are in second person. They're written in what's called a "you understood" form: even though the word *you* isn't included in this sentences, it's implied and readers understands that *you* is the subject of each sentence.)

Now let's turn to the second person. For various reasons, most instructors usually disapprove of second person in formal writing. Is using second person ever acceptable? It is when you need an informal tone or when you're writing a piece that is instructive or prescriptive. Read something written in second person (remember, that means using *you* and *your*), and you'll find a more conversational tone than if it had been written in first or third person. Use second person when you want your words to come across in a casual way. Take a look at this paragraph:

• *You'll need to watch the mixture carefully, and you may have to stir it quite often. When you get to the last step, make sure you add the final three ingredients slowly. If you add them too quickly, you'll have a mess on your hands.*

You can easily read that paragraph. It's talking directly to you, telling you what to do in your cooking. But look at the same paragraph written in third person:

- *The mixture must be watched carefully, and it may have to be stirred quite often. At the last step, it's important that the final three ingredients be added slowly. If they're added too quickly, the combination will create a mess.*

Now, that's pretty boring and stilted, isn't it? For one thing, the use of the third person makes it veer off into the passive voice, which we learned a little while back is something to be avoided if possible. The directions are far better if you write them in the second person.

Another time that second-person writing is used with frequency is in advertising. Consider this sign:

- *Come see the friendly folks at Abbotts's Used Car Lot!*

That's more inviting than if it were written in the third person:

- *Readers of this sign are invited to come see the friendly folks at Abbotts's Used Car Lot!*

The friendly folks at Abbotts's probably wouldn't have much business with a sign like that, would they?

Right: *After you're done filling out the form, you may be required to bring it to the office, where you'll have to submit it to the secretary.*

> **Wrong:** *Margaret, Elizabeth, and me were*
> *at the mall for four hours yesterday.*

Difficulties with Subjective and Objective Pronouns

Here's the first part of a no-brainer: Subjective pronouns are used as the subjects of sentences (whom or what you're talking about). You would say, for instance:

- *I am going to leave for my appointment.*

- *She is late already.*

No problem seeing the right form in those sentences, is there? For some reason, though, a problem occasionally arises when subjects are compound. You might read, for instance:

- *His brothers and him are going to the ball game.*

- *Me and her see eye to eye on lots of things.*

These pronouns are used incorrectly. Because the pronouns are used as subjects of the sentence, they should all be in the subjective case: *I, you, he, she, it, we,* or *they.* So, the sentences should read:

- *His brothers and he are going to the ball game.*

- *I and she see eye to eye on lots of things. (Actually, etiquette says to put the other person first, so it's better to word this sentence like this: She and I see eye to eye on lots of things.)*

If you're not sure if you've used the right pronoun, try writing or saying the sentence with only one subject. You'd never say:

- *Him is going to the ball game.*

- *Me sees eye to eye on lots of things.*

- *Her sees eye to eye on lots of things.*

Since those pronouns sound wrong when they're by themselves, you know that they're the wrong case. Change the pronouns to the ones you'd normally use when there's just one subject. Here's part two of the no-brainer: Objective pronouns are used as the objects in sentences. You would say, for instance:

- *Hallie and Travis went to see her last night.*

- *When Liz and Marvin celebrated their anniversary, Betty gave them a new CD.*

- *"Give me the money right now!" the robber demanded.*

As with compound subjects, problems arise with compound objects. People will write or say sentences like this:

- *The argument arose last night between Carla and she.*

- *Please buy a raffle ticket from Fr. Hammerstein, Jane Ann, or I.*

- *"The car sped by he and I, going 90 miles per hour," the witness testified.*

Again, each pronoun is used incorrectly in these sentences. Because the pronouns are used as objects, they should all be in the objective case: *me, you, him, her, it, us,* and *them.* So, the sentences should read:

- *The argument arose last night between Carla and her.*

- *Please buy a raffle ticket from Fr. Hammerstein, Jane Ann, or me.*

- *"The car sped by him and me, going 90 miles per hour," the witness testified.*

Good Grammar Tip

Remember that pronouns that are predicate nominatives should be subject pronouns. Predicate nominatives, you recall, are nouns or pronouns used after linking verbs (usually forms of *be,* like *am, is, are, was,* and *were*).

The way to test yourself if you're not sure if you've used the right pronoun is to apply the same trick that you used for the subjective pronoun problem, but substitute the objective form; that is, write or say the sentence with only one object. You'd never say:

- *The argument arose last night between she.*

- *Please buy a raffle ticket from I.*

- *"The car sped by he, going 90 miles per hour," the witness testified.*

- *"The car sped by I, going 90 miles per hour," the witness testified.*

Since those pronouns sound wrong when they're by themselves, you know that they're the wrong case. Change the pronouns to the ones you'd normally say when the sentence has only one object.

So why were *you* and *it* on the lists of both subjective and objective pronouns? Because, unlike other pronouns on the lists (*I* and *me*, for example), English uses the same form for those two words.

- *It was nice to get a surprise in the mail.*

(*It* is a subject.)

- *I got it in the mail.*

(*It* is an object.)

- *You called me at four o'clock?*

(*You* is a subject.)

- *I called you back at five o'clock.*

(*You* is an object.)

Right: *Margaret, Elizabeth, and I were at the mall for four hours yesterday.*

Wrong: *I'm looking for a big fly swatter to whack the mother of all spiders with.*

Incorrectly Ending with a Preposition

The rules of good grammar say you should avoid ending a sentence with a preposition. Of course, if you're going to do that, you need to know exactly what is meant by the term preposition, *don't you?*

It's not hard. A preposition is a word that links a noun or pronoun to some other word in a sentence. Take, for example, these short sentences:

• *Jack and Jill went up the hill.*

(*Up* is a preposition connecting *went* and *hill*.)

• *Little Jack Horner sat in a corner.*

(*In* is a preposition connecting *sat* and *corner*.)

• *Sing a song of sixpence.*

(*Of* is a preposition connecting *song* and *sixpence*.)

The most common prepositions are:

about	below	except
above	beneath	for
across	beside	from
after	between	in
against	beyond	inside
along	but	into
among	by	like
around	concerning	off
at	despite	on
before	down	onto
behind	during	out

outside	to	upon
over	toward	with
past	under	within
since	underneath	without
through	until	
throughout	up	

Some prepositions (called compound prepositions) consist of more than one word, like *in spite of, next to, on top of,* and *together with.*

Good Grammar Tip

You may remember this definition from elementary school: A preposition describes any way a mouse can go (i.e., a mouse can go *near, through, on, onto, above, along,* and so forth). This definition works for most prepositions, but not all (how can a mouse go *until, of,* or *despite?*).

If you're trying to determine if a particular word is a preposition, here's a little trick that works for many prepositions. See if the word will fit in this sentence:

- *It went _____ the thing(s).*

If the word in question makes sense in that sentence, it's a preposition. (Note that *of* is a notable exception. I'm afraid you're just going to have to remember that *of* is a preposition.)

Here's another way of remembering what a preposition is. Look at the last eight letters of the word *preposition;* they spell *position.* A preposition sometimes tells the position of something: *in, out, under, over, above,* and so forth.

Now let's get back to the rule that you should never end a sentence with a preposition. Well, sometimes that rule is correct and sometimes it isn't. Generally, your writing sounds better if you can structure a sentence so that it doesn't end with a preposition. However, sometimes you want a more colloquial or conversational tone, and—let's face it—in speaking, we often end sentences with prepositions (or should that read "a preposition is a word we often end a sentence with"?).

• *With whom are you going to the party?*

That's the "no-preposition-at-the-end" construction.

• *Whom are you going to the party with?*

That's almost the way the sentence normally is said (in fact, speakers usually use *who* instead of *whom* in a sentence like this).

So we can amend the rule as follows: Never end a sentence with a preposition unless doing so makes you sound overly formal and annoying. How's that?

Right: *I'm looking for a big fly swatter with which to whack the mother of all spiders.*

Wrong: *Having left their winter coats at home, the horses drew Peter and Sylvia along at a brisk pace through the snowstorm.*

Leaving Dangling Participles

A participle is part verb and part something else, but it's used as an adjective. Adjectives, you may remember, answer one of three questions: which one? what kind? or how many? Keep that in mind.

Some participles consist of a verb plus *-ing*, as in these sentences:

- *Let sleeping dogs lie.*

Sleeping consists of the verb *sleep* plus the ending *-ing*, and it acts as an adjective in the sentence. It describes *dogs*, and it answers the question *which ones?*

- *Shivering when they came in, Peter and Sylvia Niblo made a mad dash for the coffeepot.*

Shivering consists of the verb *shiver* plus the ending *-ing*, and it acts as an adjective in the sentence. It describes *Peter and Sylvia Niblo*, and it answers the question *what kind?* or *which one?*

The previous examples illustrate present participles.

Other participles consist of a verb plus *-d* or *-ed*, as in these sentences:

- *Exhausted by their ride through the storm, Peter and Sylvia fell asleep in front of the fire.*

Exhausted consists of the verb *exhaust* plus the ending *-ed*, and it acts as an adjective in the sentence. It describes *Peter and Sylvia*, and it answers the question *who?*

- *Stained with both mud and snow, Peter's new shirt went right into the washing machine.*

Stained consists of the verb *stain* plus the ending *-ed*, and it acts as an adjective in the sentence. It describes *shirt*, and it answers the question *which one?*

The previous examples illustrate past participles.

Good Grammar Tip

Just to complicate matters, many past participles are formed irregularly (that is, without adding -*d* or -*ed*). Some examples are *arisen, begun, chosen, dealt, gone, hurt, lain, meant,* and *outgrown.*

So what's the big deal about a participle? Sometimes it's used in the wrong way, and that creates a dangling participle (hanging participle or unattached participle). Take a look at this sentence:

• *Babbling incoherently, the nurse quickly wrapped his arms around the child.*

The way the sentence is written, the nurse was babbling (a participle) incoherently. What the writer means (at least, what we hope he or she means) is that the *child* was babbling incoherently. The sentence should be rewritten, perhaps this way:

• *The nurse quickly wrapped his arms around the babbling child.*

Here's another dangling participle:

• *Tired from her trip, the recliner looked like the perfect spot for Sylvia Niblo.*

How in the world could a recliner have a tiring trip? That participle (*tired*) and the rest of the words that go with it (its phrase: *tired from her trip*) should be moved. A better way to word that sentence would be:

• *The recliner looked like the perfect spot for Sylvia Niblo, who was tired from her trip.*

Now let's leave quietly so we don't disturb her.

Right: *The horses drew Peter and Sylvia, who had left their winter coats at home, at a brisk pace through the snowstorm.*

Wrong: *The robbers fled the bank with guns firing in every direction.*

Misplaced and Dangling Modifiers

Misplaced modifiers aren't words or phrases that are lost; they're words or phrases that you've put in the wrong place. All of your words—whether they're single words, phrases, or clauses—should be as close as possible to whatever they modify (the words they describe or elaborate on). Take a look at this sentence, written with a single word in the wrong place:

• *After her wreck, Joanna could comprehend what the ambulance driver was barely saying.*

The way the sentence is written, the ambulance driver is barely speaking—but surely that's not what the writer meant. *Barely* is out of its correct place because it modifies the wrong word. It should be moved so that it modifies the verb *could comprehend*. The sentence should be written this way:

• *After her wreck, Joanna could barely comprehend what the ambulance driver was saying.*

In addition to being single words, misplaced modifiers can also be phrases, as in this example:

• *Witnesses reported that the woman was driving the getaway car with flowing black hair.*

How interesting—a car with flowing black hair. *With flowing black hair* is in the wrong place in this sentence (it's misplaced) and should be placed after *woman*. That way, the sentence would read:

• *Witnesses reported that the woman with flowing black hair was driving the getaway car.*

Clauses, too, can be put in the wrong place, as in the following sentence:

• *Paulette Dixon couldn't stop thinking about her sick baby running in the six-mile road race.*

That's quite a baby who can run a six-mile road race (not to mention running while being sick). The clause *running in the six-mile road race* is out of place in this sentence; it should be closer to the noun it modifies (*Paulette Dixon*). The sentence should be reworded this way:

• *Running in the six-mile road race, Paulette Dixon couldn't stop thinking about her sick baby.*

Good Grammar Tip

A frequent problem often arises with the word *not*. In speaking, we frequently say something like this:

All the robbers in the car were not armed.

The problem with that blanket statement is that the word *not* may be in the wrong place. If the meaning was that some of the robbers were armed, then the sentence should be reworded this way:

Not all the robbers in the car were armed.

See that? By moving one word we've armed some of the robbers and made things more dangerous for the police trying to capture them.

One of the most common problems with misplaced modifiers comes with what are called limiting modifiers—words like *almost, even, hardly, just, merely, nearly, only* (the one misplaced most often), *scarcely*, and *simply*. To convey the correct meaning, limiting modifiers must be placed in front of the words they modify.

Take a look at these sentences:

• *Already, Mr. Goulooze has almost eaten four slabs of ribs!*

How does a person almost eat something? Did he have great willpower four different times? Or should the sentence be reworded to say that Mr. Goulooze has eaten almost four slabs of ribs?

• *Richard has nearly ruined every meal he's cooked.*

Has Richard nearly ruined every meal—in which case, he should be grateful for his luck—or has he ruined nearly every meal, in which case he probably has a lot of very unsatisfied diners?

Another common problem in writing and speaking is that of dangling modifiers. These have no word or phrase to describe; they just dangle, or hang, in a sentence without something to hold on to. Look at these sentences:

• *Long ears drooping on the floor, Julie wondered how the dog could walk.*

Is it time for Julie to consider plastic surgery to fix her ears?

• *While performing, the audience gasped as the singer forgot the words to the song.*

Why was the audience performing?

• *After getting a new paint job, reupholstering was now needed for the car.*

Why would reupholstering be painted?

Each of the sentences needs to be reworded so that the modifiers have something to attach to.

• *Julie wondered how the dog could walk with its long ears drooping on the floor.*

• *The audience gasped as the singer forgot the words to the song while he was performing.*

• *After getting a new paint job, the car needed to be reupholstered.*

Right: *The robbers, firing guns in every direction, fled the bank.*

Wrong: *And I say no way, dude, you're going to have to remake, rebox, redeliver that pizza you dropped.*

Wrong Use of Conjunctions and Interjections

A conjunction joins words in a sentence; that is, it provides a junction between words. Conjunctions are divided into three categories: coordinating, correlative, and subordinating.

Coordinating conjunctions include *and, but, or, nor, for, so,* and *yet.*

Correlative conjunctions can't stand alone; they must have a "relative" nearby, usually in the same sentence. The pairs include *both/and, either/or, neither/nor, not only/also,* and *not only/but also.*

Use **subordinating conjunctions** at the beginning of dependent (subordinate) clauses (words that have a subject and verb but can't stand alone as sentences).

Common subordinating conjunctions include:

	after	
although	how	so that
as in	if	unless
as if	in order that	until
as long as	in that	when
as much as	inasmuch as	where
as soon as	now that than	whenever
assuming that	once that	wherever
because	providing that	whether
before	since	while
even though	so long as	

Good Grammar Tip

Formal writing generally discourages the practice of beginning sentences with conjunctions. However, in informal writing or dialogue, it's okay to start a sentence with *and* or *but.* As always in writing, context is key.

Now let's turn to **interjections**.

Egads! You don't remember what an interjection is? It's a word or phrase that expresses surprise or some other emotion or is used as filler. An interjection often stands alone (*gosh, darn*). If an interjection is part of a sentence, it doesn't have a relation to other words in the sentence; if it's taken out of the sentence, the meaning is unchanged. Take a look at these sentences:

- *Hey, dude.*

- *Like, what's going on?*

- *Well, I don't know what to say.*

- *Ouch! Did you step on my toe?*

Hey, *like*, *well*, and *ouch* are interjections.

When you're expressing a strong emotion or surprise (as in *Stop!* or *Darn it all!*), use an exclamation point. If you're using milder emotion or merely using a filler (as in *like* or *well*), use a comma.

A note of caution about interjections: use them in moderation, if at all. In dialogue, interjections are used far more often than in more formal writing, where they're hardly ever used.

Good Grammar Tip

Interjections that are considered too off-color for readers are often denoted by using various symbols, in no particular order.

"I've been stood up by that $@# guy for the last time!" Lolita cried.*

Right: *I say, no way, dude! You're going to have to remake, rebox, and redeliver that pizza you dropped.*

Wrong: *Mountain climbing, I realized,*
was a sign of me getting in good shape.

Bad Use of Gerunds

A gerund is a word that begins with a verb and ends in -ing. *Wait a minute! Isn't that what a present participle is? Glad you were paying attention. Now for the rest of the story. A gerund begins with a verb, ends in* -ing, *and acts like a noun (that is, it names a person, place, or thing).*

• *Running up steep hills for the last six months has greatly improved Cathe's and Alan's stamina.*

• *Phillip and Debbie both thought they could improve their stamina by a program of taking twenty-mile hikes.*

Running is a gerund. It's composed of a verb (*run*), ends in *-ing*, and is used as a noun. *Taking* is another gerund. It's composed of a verb (*take*), ends in *-ing*, and it's used as a noun.

Good Grammar Tip

The "look at the way a word is used in a sentence" rule is especially important with verbs, participles, and gerunds. Look at the different uses of *addressing* in these sentences:

Addressing the problem made Pat Davis realize what she must do.

Addressing the audience, Donna and Jim White felt a connection as they spoke.

Anthony and Ruth Hazelwood mailed the invitations as soon as they finished addressing the envelopes.

In the first sentence, *addressing* is a gerund (a verb plus *-ing*, functioning as a noun). In the second sentence, *addressing* is a participle (a verb plus *-ing*, functioning as an adjective). In the last sentence, *addressing* is a verb (showing action).

This rule is often ignored: Use a possessive noun or possessive pronoun (*my, your, his, her, its, our,* and *their*) before a gerund. Look at this sentence:

- *David continues to be amazed by (Susan, Susan's) singing.*

Use the possessive *Susan's* before the gerund *singing.*
The same is true for this sentence:

- *Steve and Diana weren't happy about (us, our) leaving so early in the morning.*

Use the possessive pronoun *our* before the gerund *leaving.*

Right: *Mountain climbing, I realized, was a sign of my getting in good shape.*

Wrong: *To go boldly where no one has gone before.*

Misuse of Infinitives

The good news is that infinitives are easy to spot—usually. Infinitives are composed of to *plus a verb (e.g.,* to go, to carry, to drive*). Most of the time you will see infinitives used as nouns, but sometimes they crop up as adjectives or adverbs.*

- *"I want to go home!" cried the youngster.*

To go is an infinitive acting as a noun.

Hark back for a minute to your high-school English class when you were reading Shakespeare. Remember this line from *Julius Caesar*?

- *I come to bury Caesar, not to praise him.*

Okay, maybe you don't remember it. Take our word for it: *To bury* is an infinitive that acts as an adverb; it tells why I came.

- *Caesar was the first Roman ruler to die at an assassin's hand.*

To die is an infinitive that acts as an adjective; it describes *ruler*.

Now for the bad news. Sometimes the *to* part of an infinitive is omitted.

- *"Please help kill Caesar," Cassius said to Brutus.*

That sentence means the same as

- *"Please help me to kill Caesar . . . "*

Once you get used to looking at sentences in this way, you'll find that recognizing infinitives without the *to* will become automatic.

Many years ago grammarians decided that splitting an infinitive (that is, inserting a word—an adverb, to be exact—between *to* and the verb, as in *to plainly see* and *to hastily wed*) was wrong. Thankfully, that rule has gone by the wayside for all but the stuffiest editors. So for all you *Star Trek* fans, it's okay now for Captain Kirk to say that line, "To boldly go where no man has gone before!"

Why was the "no split infinitive" rule created in the first place? In the days when the study of Latin was a mandatory part of the curriculum in many schools, rules of Latin grammar often affected rules of English grammar (now, why people didn't realize Latin and English were different languages is another story altogether). Since a Latin infinitive is written as one word, it can't be split; therefore, grammarians said, the English infinitive should never be split either. To us, the enlightened ones of the twenty-first century, that dictum from days of old is an anachronism. The purpose of language, after all, is to make meaning clear.

Look at the following sentence (with a split infinitive):

- *Georgia needed to better understand the rules of English grammar.*

Now look at this sentence:

- *To really understand split infinitives, look at their construction.*

That sentence constructed without using a split infinitive would be worded like this:

- *To understand really split infinitives, look at their construction.*

or

- *Really to understand split infinitives, look at their construction.*

Those don't do justice to the meaning of the sentence, do they?

But now take a look at a sentence like this:

- *You're usually safe to make the split.*

In that instance, if you split the infinitive, you'd end up with a sentence like this:

- *You're safe to usually make the split.*

This doesn't sound right. Better to leave the infinitive whole in that case.

The moral of the story here is that you have to let your ear tell you if a split infinitive works. If it does, then by all means use it; if not, leave the infinitive alone.

Right: *To boldly go where no one has gone before.*

Wrong: *The old man carrying a large briefcase,
which he placed on a park bench.*

Getting the Subject and Predicate Wrong

*Now on to the parts of a sentence. As you probably know, a sentence can be very short
or very long. By definition, a sentence must have the following: (1) a predicate (usually
called a verb), (2) the subject of that verb, and (3) words that form a complete thought.*

The complete subject is the person, place, or thing that the sentence is
about, along with all the words that modify it (describe it or elaborate on it).
The complete predicate (verb) is what the person, place, or thing is doing, or
what condition the person, place, or thing is in.

Complete Subject	Complete Predicate (Verb)
The elderly, white-haired gentleman	*walked quickly down the hallway.*

The simple subject of a sentence is the fundamental part of the complete
subject—the main noun(s) and pronoun(s) in the complete subject. In this
example, the simple subject is *gentleman*.

The simple predicate (verb) of a sentence is the fundamental part of the
complete predicate—the verb(s) in the complete predicate. In the example,
the simple predicate is *walked*.

A sentence may also have compound subjects and predicates.

• *The elderly, white-haired gentleman and his wife walked quickly down
the hallway.*

This sentence has a compound subject: *gentleman* and *wife*.

• *The elderly, white-haired gentleman walked quickly down the hallway
and then paused to speak to me.*

This sentence has a compound verb: *walked* and *paused*.

• *The elderly, white-haired gentleman and his wife walked quickly down the
hallway and then paused to speak to me.*

This sentence has a compound subject—*gentleman* and *wife*—and a compound verb—*walked* and *paused*.

So what's wrong with the sentence at the beginning of this section?

* *The old man carrying a large briefcase, which he placed on a park bench.*

It has a subject and predicate, doesn't it? *Old man* is the subject (it's a person); *carrying* is the predicate (it's a verb). What's the problem?

Aha! You're mistaken. *Carrying* isn't a verb at all, even though its root is a verb (*carry*). Instead, it's a word describing what the old man is doing. That makes it . . . a participle! Not a verb.

Well, what about *placed*? That's a verb.

Yes, and it's trying to function as a compound verb. The problem is that it's missing the first part of the compound. That's where the problem comes in; *carrying* just isn't a verb.

Good Grammar Tip

Some sentences begin with *there* or *here* (sometimes called expletives). The inclination is to identify these expletives as subjects. But neither *here* nor *there* is a subject when used in its normal manner. A mnemonic to remember this is "The subject is neither here nor there."

If you have trouble locating the subject of a sentence, find the verb and then ask *who* or *what* did the verb. Read this sentence:

* *After a tiring morning at the gym, Justin and Michelle fell onto the floor in exhaustion.*

The verb is *fell*. If you ask, "Who or what fell?" you answer *Justin and Michelle*, which is the subject.

Remember that the subject of a sentence is never in a prepositional phrase. If the sentence is a question, the subject sometimes appears after the verb. To find the subject, turn the question around so that it resembles a declarative sentence. Then proceed in the normal way. Look at this sentence:

• *What is Willa Liberi going to do with that leftover sandwich?*

Now, turn the wording around so that you have:

• *Willa Liberi is going to do what with that leftover sandwich?*

Willa Liberi answers the *who?* or *what?* question about the verb *is going.*
Finding the subject of a sentence helps you use verbs and pronouns correctly.

Right: *The old man carried a large briefcase,*
which he placed on a park bench.

Wrong: *Mary hit when she saw her husband, Roger, flirting with the younger blonde woman.*

Misunderstanding Direct and Indirect Objects

Although some sentences are complete with only a subject and a predicate, many others need something else to complete their meaning. These additional parts of a sentence are called complements, and English has five types: direct object, object complement, indirect object, predicate adjective, and predicate nominative. Predicate adjectives and predicate nominatives are considered subject complements.

One type of complement used with a transitive verb is a **direct object**: the word or words that receive the action of the verb. Direct objects are nouns (usually), pronouns (sometimes), or noun clauses (rarely). You can find a direct object by applying this formula:

1. First, find the subject of the sentence.
2. Second, find the verb, and make sure it's transitive.
3. Third, say the subject and predicate, and then ask *whom?* or *what?* If a word answers either of those questions, it's a direct object.

All of this sounds more complicated than it is. Take a look at this sentence:

• *The little boy constantly dribbled the basketball in the outdoor playground.*

You can find the subject (*boy*) and the verb (*dribbled*), so all you do is say *boy dribbled whom or what?* The word that answers that question (*basketball*) is the direct object. Easy enough, huh?

Another kind of complement used with a transitive verb is an **object (objective) complement**; it elaborates on or gives a fuller meaning to a direct object. Object complements can be nouns, pronouns, or adjectives. Take a look at this sentence:

• *Helen and Ruth asked their sister Marie for a ride home.*

In this sentence the direct object is *Marie* (Helen and Ruth asked whom or what? *Marie*), and the noun *sister* is the object complement (it helps complete the information about the word *Marie*). Object complements that act in this way—that is, elaborate on the direct object—are nouns or pronouns.

Object complements can also be adjectives. Look at this sentence:

- *On a whim, both George and Lucy painted their fingernails blue.*

In this sentence the direct object is *fingernails* (both painted whom or what? *fingernails*), and the adjective *blue* is the object complement (it elaborates on the information about the word *fingernails*). Object complements that act in this way—that is, they describe the direct object—are adjectives.

The third type of complement used with a transitive verb is an **indirect object**. It comes before a direct object and answers the question *to whom?* or *for whom?* after the subject and verb. An easy formula for finding an indirect object is this:

1. First, find the subject of the sentence.
2. Second, find the transitive verb.
3. Third, say the subject and the predicate, and then ask *to whom?* or *for whom?* If a word answers that question, it's an indirect object.

Good Grammar Tip

In order for a sentence to have an indirect object, *to* or *for* must be implied, not stated. If either of those words is stated, then you have a prepositional phrase, not an indirect object.

Bob and Sara Payne made us a spaghetti dinner.

When you ask *Bob and Sara Payne made for whom?* the answer is *us. Us* is an indirect object.

Bob and Sara Payne made a spaghetti dinner for us.

Since *for* is in the sentence, *for us* is a prepositional phrase, not an indirect object.

Look at this example:

• *Drew reluctantly gave Courtney the keys to his new car.*

In this sentence, the subject is *Drew* and the verb is *gave*. Using the formula of asking *to whom?* or *for whom?* after the subject and verb, you would say *Drew gave to whom?* The answer is *Courtney*.

Good Grammar Tip

Not all sentences that have direct objects will have an indirect object or an object complement. You have to apply the formula to see what is in the sentence. Also, remember that if a sentence doesn't have a direct object, it can't have an object complement or an indirect object.

Other kinds of complements, called **subject complements**, are used only with linking verbs. (Linking verbs, you'll remember, are all forms of *be* and, in certain situations, *appear, become, feel, grow, look, remain, smell, sound, stay,* and *taste.*) Subject complements do just what their name implies—they complete (give you more information about) the subject. Predicate adjectives and predicate nominatives are the two types of subject complements.

Look at the example that appeared at the beginning of this section:

• *Mary hit when she saw her husband, Roger, flirting with the younger blonde woman.*

Here we have some of the elements we're looking for: *Roger* is the object complement of *husband* (that is, it gives us further information) and both are the direct object of *saw*. The problem is that *hit* is a transitive verb; that is, it must take a direct object. We can fix the problem easily with a little rewriting.

Right: *Mary hit her husband, Roger, when she saw him flirting with the younger blonde woman.*

Wrong: *The game pieces from my chess match were lying in a pile. When Mary asked me to pick them up.*

Misusing Independent and Subordinate Clauses

An independent (main) clause is a group of words that has a verb and its subject. Also, this group of words can stand alone as a sentence; that is, the words would make sense if they were by themselves. Here's an example:

- *The index cards fell to the floor.*

This is one independent clause. It has a subject (*cards*) and a verb (*fell*), and it stands alone as a sentence. Now, look at this sentence:

- *The index cards scattered on the floor, and Ora Lou and Gene had to pick them all up.*

This sentence has two independent clauses. The first—*the index cards scattered on the floor*—has a subject *cards* and a verb *scattered*; it can stand alone as a sentence. The second—*Ora Lou and Gene had to pick them all up*—has subjects (*Ora Lou* and *Gene*) and a verb (*had*); it also can stand alone as a sentence.

Good Grammar Tip

Remember that independent clauses joined by *and, but, for, or, nor, so,* or *yet* are separated by a comma. Other independent clauses are separated by a semicolon.

Now look:

- *Ora Lou and Gene had just alphabetized the index cards when the cards fell on the floor and scattered everywhere.*

The independent clause in this sentence is *Ora Lou and Gene had just alphabetized the index cards.* Although the rest of the sentence—*when the cards fell on the floor and scattered everywhere*—has a subject (*they*) and verbs (*fell* and *scattered*), it can't stand alone as a complete thought; because of this, it's not an independent clause.

A subordinate (dependent) clause has a verb and its subject, but it can't stand alone as a sentence. When you read the words of a subordinate clause, you can see a subject and a verb but the words don't make sense by themselves. In order for a subordinate clause to make sense, it has to be attached to another part (to some independent clause) of the sentence. A subordinate clause usually begins with a subordinating conjunction or a relative pronoun. Look at the last example in the discussion about independent clauses:

• *Ora Lou and Gene had just alphabetized the index cards when the cards fell on the floor and scattered everywhere.*

In this sentence, *when the cards fell on the floor and scattered everywhere* is a subordinate clause. It has a subject *the cards* and verbs *fell* and *scattered.* But read the words alone:

• *when the cards fell on the floor and scattered everywhere*

So, what about them? What happened next? If the terminology of clauses seems complicated, think of the relationship this way: Since a subordinate clause can't stand alone, it's secondary (subordinate) to the main clause of the sentence. Or, a subordinate clause relies (is dependent) on another clause (an independent clause) that's in the same sentence.

The problem with the sample sentence at the beginning of this section is that the writer has a subordinate clause (*When Mary asked me to pick them up.*) that she or he is trying to treat as its own sentence. The fix is simple enough: Just attach it to the previous sentence.

Right: *The game pieces from my chess match were lying in a pile when Mary asked me to pick them up.*

Wrong: *A man wearing a brown suit named Jones walked into the room.*

Wrong Use of Adjectival, Nominal, and Adverbial Clauses

English has three types of subordinate clauses, and each acts in a different way in a sentence.

An **adjective clause** is a subordinate clause that acts as an adjective; it modifies or describes a noun or pronoun. Looked at a different way, an adjective clause answers *which one?* or *what kind?* An adjective clause is sometimes called a relative clause because relative pronouns (*who, whose, whom, which,* and *that*) often begin adjective clauses and relate the clause to the person, place, or thing that they describe.

• *That man, whom I knew in high school, walked right by as if he'd never met me.*

Whom I knew in high school is an adjective clause. It has a verb (*knew*) and its subject (*I*), and it can't stand alone as a sentence—that's what makes it a subordinate clause. It's an adjective clause because it describes the noun *man;* in addition, it answers the question *which one?* about *man.*

Careful! Just to confuse you, sometimes an adjective clause has *that* deleted from it:

• *The new CD that Bill and Becky Brown want has not yet been released.*

• *The new CD Bill and Becky Brown want has not yet been released.*

Good Grammar Tip

Because an adjective clause modifies a noun, it can modify a subject, direct object, indirect object, predicate nominative, or object of a preposition.

A **noun clause** is a subordinate clause that acts as a noun; it can be the subject, predicate nominative, appositive, object of a verb, or object of a preposition. A noun clause answers *who? whom?* or *what?*

- *Kevin, Lynda, and Mike couldn't believe what they heard at the library.*

What they heard at the library is a noun clause. It has a subject (*they*) and a verb (*heard*) and it can't stand alone as a sentence, so it's some type of subordinate clause. Because it's the direct object of *couldn't believe* (and therefore functions in the sentence as a noun), it's a noun clause.

Good Grammar Tip

A noun clause is often introduced by *if, how, that, what, whatever, when, where, whether, which, who, whoever, whom, whomever, whose,* or *why.*

An **adverb clause** is a subordinate clause that acts as an adverb; it can modify or describe a verb, an adjective, or another adverb. Looked at in a different way, an adverb clause answers *when? where? how? why? to what extent? with what goal or result?* or *under what condition or circumstances?* An adverb clause is introduced by a subordinating conjunction, such as *after, although, as (if), because, once, until,* and *while.* For example:

- *Mr. Kasenow visited Kim because he was attracted to her.*

Because he was attracted to her is an adverb clause. It has a subject (*he*) and a verb (*was attracted*). It can't stand alone as a sentence, so it's some type of subordinate clause. Because it modifies the verb *visited*, it's an adverb clause.

Remember to use a comma after an introductory adverb clause, as in this example:

- *Whenever he came to visit, Mr. Kasenow brought Kim a box of candy.*

Good Grammar Tip

Ever wonder what's the difference between a phrase and a clause? A clause has a verb and its subject; a phrase doesn't.

The sample sentence at the beginning of this section contains an adjective clause:

• *A man wearing a brown suit named Jones walked into the room.*

However, there's a problem with it. Can you spot it? Of course. The suit wasn't named Jones; the man was. A simple bit of rearranging and the addition of a couple of commas fixes the problem.

> **Right:** *A man named Jones, wearing a brown suit, walked into the room.*

[Part IV]

Misfiring Sentences (and How to Fix Them)

Wrong: *On the long road ahead we must travel together, we can work as one, and you will need to be determined.*

Lack of Parallel Construction

For your work to be easily read—and, in some cases, for it to be coherent—using parallelism is important. This helps you give equality and balance to the separate points you make.

Puzzled? Not to worry. Understanding parallelism isn't as difficult as it may seem. You simply write all the similar parts of a sentence in the same way. If you've used two nouns, you don't suddenly switch to a gerund. If you've used verbs that have a certain tense, you don't suddenly change tenses. If you begin in one voice, you don't suddenly switch to another voice.

Here are some famous lines that use parallelism effectively:

• *"With this faith we will be able to work together, to pray together, to struggle together, to go to jail together, to stand up for freedom together, knowing that we will be free one day."—Rev. Martin Luther King Jr.*

• *"I came, I saw, I conquered."—Julius Caesar*

Take a look at some of the examples that follow, and you'll get a clearer understanding of what parallelism is and how important it is in your writing.

Parallelism Problem #1: Items in Pairs or in a Series. When naming items, you should present them all in the same way. Look at this problem sentence:

• *This afternoon Doris and Stefanie washed and waxed, and then they were vacuuming the car.*

Here is the problem viewed one way:

• *This afternoon Doris and Stefanie washed (past tense verb) and waxed (past tense verb), and then they were vacuuming (past progressive tense verb) the car.*

Here is the problem viewed another way:

• *This afternoon Doris and Stefanie washed (-ed word) and waxed (-ed word), and then they were vacuuming (-ing word) the car.*

Here's the repaired sentence that's now parallel:

• *This afternoon Doris and Stefanie washed, waxed, and vacuumed the car.*

All the verbs are now in the same tense; all verbs are now *-ed* words.

The following example shows the incorrect use of parallel items in a series when a colon is used:

• *A word processor has three helpful features that save time: you can quickly edit material you don't want, you can save drafts and revise them, and it can automatically correct words that you frequently misspell.*

Here's the problem viewed one way:

• *A word processor has three helpful features that save time: you (second person) can quickly edit material you don't want, you (second person) can save drafts and revise them, and it (third person) can automatically correct words that you frequently misspell.*

Here's the problem viewed another way:

• *A word processor has three helpful features that save time: you (you as subject) can quickly edit material you don't want, you (you as subject) can save drafts and revise them, and it (it as subject) can automatically correct words that you frequently misspell.*

Here's the repaired sentence that's now parallel:

• *A word processor has three helpful features that save time: you can quickly edit material you don't want, you can save drafts and revise them, and you can automatically correct words that you frequently misspell.*

Parallelism Problem #2: Clauses. When you're using more than one clause, keep the same voice and use the same type of introduction in each. Here's the problem sentence:

• *I was worried that Joan would drive too fast, that the road would be too slippery, and that the car would be stopped by the police.*

Here's the problem viewed one way:

• *I was worried that Joan would drive too fast (active voice), that the road would be too slippery (active voice), and that the car would be stopped by the police (passive voice).*

Here's the repaired sentence that's now parallel:

• *I was worried that Joan would drive too fast, that the road would be too slippery, and that the police would stop the car.*

Now look at this problem sentence:

• *Mary Elizabeth and Ron promised that they would bring everything for the picnic, that they would be on time, and not to forget the bug repellent.*

This is one way to look at the problem:

• *Mary Elizabeth and Ron promised that they would bring everything for the picnic (clause introduced with a subordinating conjunction), that they would be on time (clause introduced with a subordinating conjunction), and not to forget the bug repellent (clause introduced with an adverb and infinitive).*

Or you can look at it this way:

• *Mary Elizabeth and Ron promised that they would bring everything for the picnic (clause introduced with* that*), that they would be on time (clause introduced with* that*), and not to forget the bug repellent (clause introduced with* not to forget*).*

Here's the repaired sentence that's now parallel:

• *Mary Elizabeth and Ron promised that they would bring everything for the picnic, that they would be on time, and that they wouldn't forget the bug repellent.*

Parallelism Problem #3: Placement. Items in a series should be placed in similar locations. Take a look at this problem sentence:

- *Mike is not only very kind but also is very good-looking.*

Let's look at the problem:

- *Mike is not only (first part of a correlative conjunction* not only *comes after the verb) very kind but also (second part of a correlative conjunction* but also *comes before the verb) is very good-looking.*

Here's the repaired sentence that's now parallel:

- *Mike is not only very kind but also very good-looking.*

Parallelism Problem #4: Placement of Emphasis or Chronology. If the items in a list have different degrees of importance or if they occur at different times, you should order them according to their emphasis or chronology. Look at this problem sentence:

- *Misuse of the drug can result in fever, death, or dizziness.*

Now, identify the problem:

- *Misuse of the drug can result in fever (something that's bad), death (something that's the worst of the three), or dizziness (something that's bad).*

Here's the repaired sentence that's now parallel:

- *Misuse of the drug can result in fever, dizziness, or death.*

In writing your sentence this way you've built up to the climax (the worst problem—death). You might also include a word or phrase before the last element to add to the buildup; for example, you could word the sentence like this:

- *Misuse of the drug can result in fever, dizziness, or even death.*

Parallelism Problem #5: Missing Words. Be sure to include all the words you need for each item in your sentence. Look at this problem sentence:

• *Coach Tom Todd was honored for guiding his star player Cathy Rymer in her career, her schoolwork, and faith.*

Identify the problem:

• *Coach Tom Todd was honored for guiding his star player Cathy Rymer in her career, her schoolwork, and faith* (*the word* her *is not included in the last item of the list of how the coach guided Rymer*).

Here's the repaired sentence that's now parallel:

• *Coach Tom Todd was honored for guiding his star player Cathy Rymer in her career, her schoolwork, and her faith.*

Parallelism Problem #6: Unclear Meaning. Include all the words necessary to indicate the items to which you're referring in the sentence. Look at this problem sentence:

• *In conducting her interview, Gail Bushrod talked with the college senior and candidate for the job.*

Identify the problem: Did Gail talk with one person who was a senior and who was interviewing for the job, or with two people—one of whom was a senior and one of whom was interviewing for the job?

Here's the repaired sentence that's now parallel:

• *In conducting her interview, Gail Bushrod talked with both the college senior and the candidate for the job.*

Parallelism Problem #7: Too Many Words. You don't need to repeat the same introductory word if it applies to all of the items in your list. Look at this problem sentence:

• *Bill hopes to see Randa on November 20, December 13, and on January 7.*

Identify the problem:

- *Bill hopes to see Randa on (preposition before noun) November 20, (preposition missing) December 13, and on (preposition appears again) January 7.*

Here's the repaired sentence that's now parallel:

- *Bill hopes to see Randa on November 20, December 13, and January 7.*

The same preposition (*on*) relates to each date, so there is no need to repeat it.

Good Grammar Tip

Sometimes you may deliberately repeat certain elements of your sentence:

I promise to cut taxes, spending, and exorbitant salary raises.

That sentence is fine the way it is, but to add emphasis to the cuts, you might choose to write it this way:

I promise to cut taxes, to cut spending, and to cut exorbitant salary raises.

Parallelism Problem #8: Too Few Words. If different prepositions apply to items in a series, be sure to include all the prepositions. Look at this problem sentence:

- *The ants are on the living-room floor, the dining-room table, and the sink. (Yikes! Better get out the bug spray!)*

Identify the problem:

- *The ants are on (use the preposition* on *with this phrase) the floor, (use the preposition* on *with this phrase) the kitchen table, and (use the preposition* on *with this phrase, but the preposition should be* in*) the sink.*

Here's the repaired sentence that's now parallel:

- *The ants are on the living-room floor, on the dining-room table, and in the sink.*

The beginning preposition (*on*) doesn't relate to each area, so you should repeat it in the second phrase and change it to *in* for the third phrase.

Parallelism Problem #9: Parallel Sentences. To add emphasis or smoothness, construct your sentences in a parallel way. Look at this example:

• *I was nervous and frightened, and I hid my emotions. My sister showed the world that she felt confident and carefree.*

Identify the problem: Actually, there's no grammatical problem with the sentences, but they can certainly be improved by being written in a parallel manner.

Here are the repaired sentences that are now parallel:

• *I was nervous and frightened, and I hid my emotions. My sister was confident and carefree, and she showed the world how she felt.*

If a lack of parallelism is often a problem in your writing, try the following tips:

- Look for *-ing* or *-ed* constructions.
- Look for constructions beginning with *it, that, to,* and *you*.
- Look for constructions beginning with the same preposition.
- Look at the voice (active or passive) used in the constructions.
- Check to see if one of the constructions is more important than the others; if so, place it last.
- If you've used a correlative conjunction, check to see if you have its partner (e.g., *either . . . or*).
- If you have items in a series, write them down in a column. Look for common elements in two parts of the series, and then convert the other items so they'll be formed in the same way. Sometimes your ear is more reliable than your eye. Good writers read their material aloud and listen for words and phrases that aren't parallel.

Right: *On the long road ahead we must travel together, we can be determined and work as one.*

Wrong: *The new breath mint assures customers that it will last all day.*

Faulty Predication and Coordination

Making sure your sentences are inherently logical is one of the most important steps in becoming a good writer. You can be quite meticulous in crafting the grammar and punctuation of your sentences and very careful with your spelling and word usage, but if your material has errors in logic, all your hard work will have been for nothing. Lapses in logic can take several different forms. Some are instantly recognizable in a sentence, while others are a little more subtle and, thus, a little more dangerous. Don't let these errors sneak up on you. As you write, keep the following common mistakes in mind.

Faulty predication (also called illogical predication or—are you ready for this one?—selectional restriction violation) is one type of illogical writing. The term *faulty predication* means that your subject and verb don't make sense together—that is, the subject can't "be" or "do" the verb.

Take a look at these sentences:

- *An economics class is when you study monetary and fiscal policy.*

- *In tennis, "playing the net" is where you stand close to the net and hit balls before they bounce.*

- *The reason Felicia Sanners was late was because she had a flat tire.*

Each of these sentences has an example of faulty predication. Obviously, a class isn't *when* anything; playing the net isn't *where* anything; and a reason isn't *because* anything. Each of these sentences needs to be reworded, perhaps like this:

- *In an economics class you study monetary and fiscal policy.*

- *In tennis, "playing the net" means you stand close to the net and hit balls before they bounce.*

- *The reason Felicia Sanners was late was that she had a flat tire.*

Good Grammar Tip

The illogical uses of *when* and *where* are two of the most common examples of faulty predication. Don't describe a noun or pronoun by using *when* or *where*. Be sure to check your sentence every time (that is, whenever and wherever) you use *when* or *where*.

To check for faulty predication, ask yourself if it's possible for each subject to "do" or "be" the verb. If it's not possible, then change your wording.

Faulty coordination occurs if you join (combine or coordinate) two clauses in an illogical way:

• *Joey and Micah made their way to the head of the checkout line, yet Joey realized he had forgotten his wallet.*

The word *yet* (the word that joins, combines, or coordinates the two clauses) is used incorrectly. The sentence could read:

• *Joey and Micah made their way to the head of the checkout line, but then Joey realized he had forgotten his wallet.*

Another example of faulty coordination comes in sentences that contain independent clauses of unequal importance. The sentences are written in a way that makes the clauses seem equal, as in the following sentence:

• *David and Kathy paid $50,000 for their new car, and it has tinted glass.*

The cost of the car is much more important than the fact that it has tinted glass (at least, it is to most people). To correct the problem, you could make the second clause subordinate to the first (making the second clause an adjective clause):

• *David and Kathy paid $50,000 for their new car, which has tinted glass.*

One common problem with comparison occurs when you use absolute adjectives, which are words that—by their definition—can't be compared. *Round*, for instance, is one of those words. Something is either round or it's not. Since one thing can't be rounder than something else, *round* is an absolute adjective.

Other absolute adjectives include these:

blank	pure
complete	square
dead	straight
empty	true
eternal	unanimous
favorite	unique
permanent	vacant

Look at these examples:

• *The test paper I turned in was somewhat blank.*

You can't have a paper that is somewhat blank; either it has something on it or it doesn't.

• *This is my most favorite restaurant.*

Because *favorite* means *at the top of my list,* one place can't be more favorite than someplace else.

Since these words can't be compared, be sure not to use *more, most, quite, rather, somewhat, very,* and other qualifiers in front of them.

Faulty comparison occurs if you compare two unlike people, places, or things:

• *The traffic mishaps in April were more numerous than May.*

This sentence compares mishaps to May, which makes no sense. The sentence should be rewritten like this:

• *The traffic mishaps in April were more numerous than those in May.*

Take a look at this one:

• *Jeff Eichholtz came to the conclusion that the people in Crydonville are friendlier than Park City.*

Here people are being compared to a city—obviously, an illogical comparison. The sentence needs to be reworded, perhaps like this:

- *Jeff Eichholtz came to the conclusion that the people in Crydonville are friendlier than the people in Park City.*

Still another problem is an ambiguous comparison, which occurs if you write a statement that could be interpreted two different ways. Look at this sentence:

- *Dawn dislikes traveling alone more than Dave.*

This is an ambiguous comparison because readers aren't sure what the word *more* applies to. Does Dawn dislike traveling alone more than she dislikes Dave, or does she dislike traveling more than Dave does?

Sweeping (hasty) generalizations use all-encompassing words like *anyone, everyone, always, never, everything, all, only,* and *none,* and superlatives like *best, greatest, most, least.*

- *The country never recovers from an economic downturn in just six months.*

Be careful with sentences with generalizations like this one. What happens to the writer's credibility if the country does, in fact, recover from a downturn in six months? You're far better off writing in terms of what happens *most of the time* than in terms of what *always* or *never* happens (not to mention that you're protected when you make a mistake). One rewording of the example is this:

- *The country almost never recovers from an economic downturn in just six months.*

Here's another example of a sweeping generalization:

- *Everyone should strenuously exercise at least thirty minutes a day.*

Everyone? Surely a newborn baby or someone who's recovering from surgery shouldn't strenuously exercise. If you reword the sentence, you can leave some room for exceptions or for debate. Here's a rewording that is more reasonable:

- *Everyone who is able should exercise at least thirty minutes a day.*

A **non sequitur** is a problem in logic that states an effect that doesn't follow its cause. Put another way, in a non sequitur, the inference or conclusion that you assert doesn't logically follow from what you previously stated.

- *I turned in a paper; therefore, I'll pass the class.*

As any teacher can tell you, the fact that you turned in a paper doesn't necessarily mean you'll pass the class. What if the paper is (a) not on the assigned topic? (b) too short or too long? (c) plagiarized? (d) three weeks late? (e) written on a kindergarten level? In other words, just because one thing happened, the other doesn't necessarily follow. Here are other examples of non sequiturs:

- *Charlie Buckman has bought products made by Commonwealth Foods for years.*

- *Jack Spratt stole a box of paper clips from the office. He probably cheats on his taxes, too.*

- *Jamecka Green is our representative in Congress. Certainly we can trust her.*

Right: *The makers of the new breath mint assure customers that the mint will last all day.*

Wrong: *Scared stiff by the intense wind and storm.*

Annoying Sentence Fragments

Fragments and run-ons can significantly weaken your writing, confusing your readers and preventing you from getting your point across. But don't let these problems scare you. By this time you've already mastered so many points of grammar and style that you'll probably find gaining the upper hand over fragments and run-ons to be a piece of cake!

You've been told time and again not to use sentence fragments. Right? (Notice that fragment?) Generally speaking, you shouldn't use fragments because they can confuse your reader, and they sometimes don't get your point across.

How can you recognize fragments? The textbook definition says that a fragment is "a group of words that isn't a sentence." Okay, so what constitutes a sentence? Again, the textbook definition says a sentence is a group of words that (1) has a subject, (2) has a predicate (verb), and (3) expresses a complete thought.

Good Grammar Tip

Depending on when and where you went to school, you might be more familiar with the definition that says a sentence must form an independent clause. Actually, an independent clause must have a subject, predicate, and complete thought, so the definitions are the same.

If a string of words doesn't have all three of the qualifications (a subject, a verb, and an expression of a complete thought), then you have a fragment rather than a sentence. That's pretty straightforward, don't you think? Take a look at these two words:

• *Spot ran.*

You have a subject (*Spot*), a verb (*ran*), and the words express a complete thought; in other words, you don't get confused when you read the two words by themselves. Since you have all the requirements (subject, verb, complete thought), you have a sentence.

Now, look at this group of words:

- *Although Christian Hazelwood had a new job in a modern office building.*

This example is a subordinate clause that's punctuated as if it were a sentence. You have a subject (*Christian Hazelwood*) and a verb (*had*), but what you don't have is a complete thought. The words serve only to introduce the main idea of the sentence. If someone said only those words to you, you'd be left hanging because you wouldn't know what the main idea was. (*Although Christian Hazelwood had a new job*—what? He took off for the Far East? He called in sick on his first day? He decided to elope with a billionaire and never have to work again?) The *although* that introduces the sentence means there should be something else to explain the first group of words.

A participial phrase often creates another common sentence fragment. Look at this example:

- *Going to the beach with her family and friends.*

This groups of words doesn't have a main clause to identify who or what is being talked about. Who was going to the beach? Obviously, something's missing.

If you're not sure if the words you've used constitute a sentence, first write them by themselves and then ask yourself if they can be understood without something else being added. If you're still not sure, let them get cold for a while and then reread them. If you're *still* not sure, call a friend and say those particular words and nothing else. You know you have a fragment if your friend says something along the lines of, "And then what?"

Another good way to see if you have a fragment is to take the word group and turn it into a yes-or-no question. If you answer yes to the question, you have a sentence; if you answer no (or if the question makes no sense), you have a fragment. Look at these examples:

- *Jordan Hill quickly ran back to the shelter of the mansion.*

Did Jordan Hill quickly run back to the shelter of the mansion? Yes, he did. Therefore, you have a sentence.

- *Scared stiff by the intense wind and storm.*

Did scared stiff by the intense wind and storm? No, that doesn't make sense. You have a fragment.

Read the following paragraph and see if you can spot the fragments:

* *The lone woman trudged up the muddy riverbank. Determined that she would make the best of a bad situation. Because of her family's recent run of bad luck. She knew that she had to contribute to the family's finances. That's why she had accepted a teaching position. In this town that was new to her. Impatiently waiting for someone to show her where she was to live. She surveyed the streets and rundown buildings of the little village. Little did she know the problems that she would face in the "wilderness," as she had mentally thought of her new home. First, the schoolhouse wasn't ready. Even though she had written that she wanted to begin classes on the twenty-fourth. The day after her arrival.*

Did you spot all the fragments? Take a look at:

* *Determined that she would make the best of a bad situation.*

* *Because of her family's recent run of bad luck.*

* *In this town that was new to her.*

* *Impatiently waiting for someone to show her where she was to live.*

* *Even though she had written that she wanted to begin classes on the twenty-fourth.*

* *The day after her arrival.*

If you had those words alone on a piece of paper, would anybody know what you meant? No—those words don't form complete thoughts.

Now, how can you correct these fragments? Usually the fragment should be connected to the sentence immediately before or after it—whichever sentence the fragment refers to. (A word of caution: Just be sure that the newly created sentence makes sense.)

The first fragment (*Determined that she would make the best of a bad situation*) can be corrected by hooking it on to the sentence right before it. The corrected sentence should read:

• *The lone woman trudged up the muddy riverbank, determined that she would make the best of a bad situation.*

You could also put the fragment at the beginning of a sentence:

• *Determined that she would make the best of a bad situation, the lone woman trudged up the muddy riverbank.*

Or you could put the fragment inside the sentence:

• *The lone woman, determined that she would make the best of a bad situation, trudged up the muddy riverbank.*

Each of these three new sentences makes sense.

Now, look at the second fragment: *Because of her family's recent run of bad luck.* What about their run of bad luck? Again, if you said those words— and only those words—to someone, you'd get a blank stare; you didn't give the reason behind the *because.* To correct this fragment, you could tack the fragment onto the beginning or middle of the sentence that follows it in the original paragraph:

• *Because of her family's recent run of bad luck, Elizabeth knew that she had to contribute to the family's finances.*

• *Elizabeth knew that, because of her family's recent run of bad luck, she had to contribute to the family's finances.*

By slightly changing some wording (without changing the meaning), you could also add this fragment to the end of the sentence:

• *Elizabeth knew that she had to contribute to her family's finances because of her parents' recent run of bad luck.*

Here's another example of possibilities for rewording a sentence when you incorporate a fragment. Take this fragment and its related sentence:

• *Impatiently waiting for someone to show her where she was to live. Elizabeth surveyed the village.*

You might reword the fragment and sentence and combine them this way:

• *Elizabeth surveyed the village as she waited impatiently for someone to show her where she was to live.*

Another way you might revise is to create an appositive phrase. Take this combination of a sentence and two fragments:

• *The schoolhouse wasn't ready. Even though Elizabeth Blackwell had written that she wanted to begin classes on the twenty-fourth. The day after her arrival.*

It can be rewritten to read:

• *The schoolhouse wasn't ready even though Elizabeth Blackwell had written that she wanted to begin classes on the twenty-fourth, the day after her arrival.*

Here, *the day after her arrival* functions as an appositive phrase.

Formal writing generally doesn't permit you to use fragments; however, using fragments in casual writing is okay—if they don't confuse your reader. Remember that using fragments (even sparingly) depends on your audience, the restrictions of your instructor or company, and your personal writing style.

You might use fragments in short stories or novels (you've started your Great American Novel, haven't you?). A rule of thumb is that you shouldn't use them too often and you certainly shouldn't use them in any way that would puzzle your readers.

Rarely—if ever—should you use a fragment in a news story in a magazine or newspaper. If, however, you're writing an editorial, a fragment might be just what you need to get your point across.

• *Do we need the new tax that's on the ballot? Without a doubt. Will it pass? Probably not.*

Both *Without a doubt* and *Probably not* are fragments. But look at how much punch you lose if you worded that passage with complete sentences instead of fragments:

• *Do we need the new tax that's on the ballot? Without a doubt we do. Will it pass? No, it probably will not.*

Good Grammar Tip

Remember that you may use fragments if you're quoting someone; in fact, you *must* use fragments if that's what the speaker used.

Fragments are also acceptable in bulleted or numbered lists. Take a look at the following example:

• *Acceptable uses of a fragment include the following:*
  • *When you're quoting someone*
  • *In a bulleted or numbered list*
  • *To make a quick point—but only when the construction isn't confusing to readers*

Taken individually, each of the bullets is a fragment, but its meaning is clear. In the type of writing that you do, if you're permitted (or even encouraged) to include bulleted lists, then using fragments is fine.

Good Grammar Tip

You'll often see fragments as titles, captions, or headings; that's generally acceptable because space restrictions usually won't allow complete sentences. Fragments are also frequently used in advertising. Since fragments are short, readers probably remember them more easily than they would complete sentences.

Sometimes you'll see a fragment intentionally used for emphasis or wry humor. Look at the title of this section and you'll see words that were deliberately constructed as fragments. Also, take a look at this example:

• *Charlotte Critser quickly told the prospective employer she would never accept a job in a city more than a hundred miles from her hometown. Never.*

Under no circumstances. For no amount of money. Well, maybe for a new car, an expense account, and double her current salary.

Now let's fix that sentence we encountered at the start of this section. While we're at it, we might as well take the opportunity to give a couple of people some fun.

Right: *Scared stiff by the intense wind and storm, Marie and David dived into a hut and made out until the tempest abated.*

Wrong: *Mark and Phil felt that Peter was being old-fashioned in his outlook, Peter thought they were irresponsible.*

Run-On Sentences

Another mistake in sentence construction is the run-on sentence. The term run-on *simply means that your sentence has at least two complete thoughts (two independent clauses, if your mind thinks that way), but it lacks the necessary punctuation between the thoughts. This punctuation is needed for readers to know when one thought stops and another begins. Consider the following sentence:*

- *The punctuation code gives your readers a signal about where one thought stops and another begins if you don't use some code your readers will be confused.*

Say what? Instead of having the needed punctuation between *begins* and *if*, the sentence, well, "runs on" and its meaning is unclear. (A fairly simple concept, wouldn't you say?)

One type of run-on, called a fused sentence, occurs when two or more sentences are written (fused) together without a punctuation mark to show readers where the break occurs. Take a look at this sentence:

- *For our annual picnic, Chris Doss and Brad Cummings brought hamburgers we brought potato salad.*

This sentence has two separate thoughts:

- *For our annual picnic, Chris Doss and Brad Cummings brought hamburgers*

and

- *we brought potato salad.*

This sentence needs some punctuation to tell readers where one thought ends and another begins. You may do this in one of three ways:

1. By creating two separate sentences (*For our annual picnic, Chris Doss and Brad Cummings brought hamburgers. We brought potato salad.*)

2. By inserting a semicolon (*For our annual picnic, Chris Doss and Brad Cummings brought hamburgers; we brought potato salad.*)
3. By inserting a comma and one of seven conjunctions—*but, or, yet, so, for, and, nor* (*For our annual picnic, Chris Doss and Brad Cummings brought hamburgers, and we brought potato salad.*)

Good Grammar Tip

Remember that you must have two (or more) complete thoughts in order to correct a run-on sentence. Ask yourself if each group of words could stand alone (that is, could be a sentence by itself). If one group of words doesn't make sense as a sentence, then you don't have a complete thought.

Another type of run-on is a comma splice (comma fault), a sentence that has two complete thoughts that are joined (spliced together) by just a comma. The problem with a comma splice is that the comma should be replaced by something else—a different punctuation mark, additional words, or both. Take a look at this sentence:

• *Rachel Johnson wanted to go to the ball game, her friend Kelly Estes wanted to see the new movie.*

On either side of the comma, you have a complete thought. The punctuation code says that you need something stronger than just a comma to help readers understand that a thought has been completed.

You have several choices to correct the sentence. You could create two separate sentences by using a period:

• *Rachel Johnson wanted to go to the ball game. Her friend Kelly Estes wanted to see the new movie.*

Another option is to separate the two complete thoughts with a semicolon:

• *Rachel Johnson wanted to go to the ball game; her friend Kelly Estes wanted to see the new movie.*

A third choice is to separate the two complete thoughts with a semicolon and a connecting word or phrase:

• *Rachel Johnson wanted to go to the ball game; however, her friend Kelly Estes wanted to see the new movie.*

Or you could join the two sentences by leaving in the comma but adding one of the seven *boysfan* conjunctions (*but, or, yet, so, for, and, nor*). Of course, you may use the conjunctions only if the sentence makes sense. You may have:

• *Rachel Johnson wanted to go to the ball game, but her friend Kelly Estes wanted to see the new movie.*

Good Grammar Tip

A comma splice frequently occurs with two quoted sentences, as in this example:

"We're going to the theater at seven," Katrina Rose said "I'd better get dressed right now."

Katrina stated two separate sentences, so you should use either a period (preferable in this case) or a semicolon after *said*.

Another way you can correct either a fused sentence or a comma splice is to reword the sentence so that one part becomes subordinate (that is, it can't stand alone as a complete thought). Let's look at the first example:

• *For our annual picnic, Chris Doss and Brad Cummings brought hamburgers we brought potato salad.*

You might reword this in a number of ways:

• *While Chris Doss and Brad Cummings brought hamburgers for our annual picnic, we brought potato salad.*

or

• *Whereas Chris Doss and Brad Cummings brought hamburgers for our annual picnic, we brought potato salad.*

Yes, this one sounds really stuffy, and you probably wouldn't use it because of its style—but it does make sense.

Now look at the second example:

• *Rachel Johnson wanted to go to the ball game, her friend Kelly Estes wanted to see the new movie.*

You could rewrite it in this way:

• *Although Rachel Johnson wanted to go to the ball game, her friend Kelly Estes wanted to see the new movie.*

or

• *While Rachel Johnson wanted to go to the ball game, her friend Kelly Estes wanted to see the new movie.*

In each of these examples the first part of the rewritten sentence (the part before the comma) can't stand alone as a sentence.

Right: *Mark and Phil felt that Peter was being old-fashioned in his outlook, while Peter thought they were irresponsible.*

Wrong: *I liked Angela. I asked her on a date.*
It didn't work out.

Misusing Connectors

Good writers rely on the use of transitional words and phrases (connecting words or parenthetical expressions). Transitional words and phrases show your readers the association between thoughts, sentences, or paragraphs; plus, they help make your writing smoother.

Sometimes sentences and paragraphs have perfectly constructed grammar, punctuation, and usage, but they lack transitional words or phrases. Material written that way seems awkward and stiff, as in this example:

• *The blind date was a disaster. It was a complete debacle. I was intrigued by what my "friend" Sarah had told me about Bill; she had said he was charming and was open to meeting someone new. He had recently seen me at a party and had wanted to meet me. Sarah said Bill was just my type. She said he was an avid reader; we would have lots to talk about. He liked playing tennis; that was a plus for me.*

There's nothing wrong with the grammar, punctuation, or spelling in that paragraph, but it's choppy and boring. Now read the same paragraph after transitional words and phrases (underlined) have been added:

• *The blind date was <u>more</u> than a disaster. <u>Actually</u>, it was <u>clearly</u> a complete debacle. <u>At first</u>, I was <u>somewhat</u> intrigued by what my "friend" Sarah had told me about Bill; <u>namely</u>, she had said he was quite charming and was open to meeting someone new. <u>In fact</u>, he had recently seen me <u>in the distance</u> at a party and had wanted to meet me. <u>Besides</u>, Sarah said, Bill was just my type. She said he was <u>quite</u> an avid reader <u>for one thing; therefore</u>, we would have lots to talk about. <u>In addition</u>, he liked playing tennis; that was <u>certainly</u> a plus for me.*

Much better, isn't it? By including the transitions, the movement from one idea to another is much smoother, and the language of the paragraph has some life in it.

As important as transitions are in sentences, they're equally important between paragraphs. (Do you see how that transition sentence connects the idea of the preceding paragraph with the idea of this one?) These transitions help you move smoothly from one major concept to the next one.

The following is an excerpt from a piece that compares an essay titled "Why Would You . . . ?" to a personal experience of the writer. Read the two paragraphs and pay particular attention to the first sentence of the second paragraph, the transitional sentence.

• *In Conrad Allen's essay "Why Would You . . . ?" the author recounts how he had been humiliated in elementary school. Allen had been infatuated with Mandy Grayson, a pretty, pigtailed little girl in his class. One Valentine's Day, Allen gave Mandy a card with "Manndy" perfectly printed—if incorrectly spelled—on the envelope. After she tore open the card, Mandy glanced at it and, much to Conrad's dismay, let it drop on the floor. In a voice loud enough for all the class to hear, she said to Conrad, "Why would you give me a card? You're too dumb and ugly." Allen writes that he first felt his face turn red in embarrassment, and then he felt complete humiliation as the whole class turned around to stare at him to see his reaction. All he could do was stand frozen in front of Mandy, trying in vain to hold back his shame and his tears.*

• *Like Allen, I felt shame when I was young. When I was in the fifth grade, my family was undergoing some difficult times. At that age, I was close friends with a group of four other girls; in fact, we called ourselves the "Live Five." Because we all had the same teacher, we were able to spend recess and lunchtime together, and we frequently spent the night at each other's houses as well. At one of the sleepovers at my house, the Live Five vowed to stay up all night. Big mistake. In our efforts to keep each other awake, we disturbed my father. That night happened to be one of the many when he was drunk, and he came down to the basement and began cursing and screaming at all of my friends. Not only did he say horrible things to me, but he also yelled at each of my friends and called them terrible names. The shame of that night continues with me today whenever I see one of the Live Five.*

Wow, get out the tissues! In reading these tearjerkers, you probably noticed that the sentence at the beginning of the second paragraph provides a connection between the ideas of the first paragraph and second paragraph. The first two words (*Like Allen*) signal that the main idea of the first paragraph will be continued and that a comparison will be made. Plus, the rest of the sentence (*I felt shame in school*) gives a clue about the topic of the second paragraph. If the transition sentence weren't there, and the second paragraph began *When I was in the fifth grade . . .* , the second paragraph would seem disjointed from the first, and readers would be confused.

Good Grammar Tip

Remember that transitional phrases are usually enclosed in commas, unless they're necessary to the meaning of a sentence.

As you can see from these examples (that's another transitional phrase— but you picked up on that, didn't you?), you should add transitions whenever possible to provide necessary links between thoughts and between paragraphs. By using them, your writing becomes much more unified and articulate.

Transitional words and phrases can be divided into categories, grouped according to their use. The following should give you lots of ideas for adding transitional elements to your writing:

- **Addition/sequence:** *additionally, afterward, again, also, and, and then, another . . . , besides, equally important, eventually, finally, first . . . second . . . third, further, furthermore, in addition, in the first place, initially, last, later, likewise, meanwhile, moreover, next, other, overall, still, too, what's more*
- **Concession:** *admittedly, although it's true that, certainly, conceding that, granted that, in fact, it may appear that, naturally, no doubt, of course, surely, undoubtedly, without a doubt*
- **Contrast:** *after all, alternatively, although, and yet, at the same time, but, conversely, despite, even so, even though, for all that, however, in contrast, in spite of, instead, nevertheless, nonetheless, nor, notwithstanding, on the contrary, on the other hand, or, otherwise, regardless, still, though, yet*
- **Examples, clarification, emphasis:** *after all, an instance of this, as an illustration, by all means, certainly, clearly, definitely, e.g., even, for example, for instance, for one thing, i.e., importantly, indeed, in fact, in other words, in particular, in short, more than that, namely, of course, of major concern, once again, specifically, somewhat, such as, that is, that is to say, the following example, this can be seen in, thus, to clarify,*

to demonstrate, to illustrate, to repeat, to rephrase, to put another way, truly, undoubtedly, without a doubt

- **Place or direction:** *above, adjacent to, at that point, below, beyond, close by, closer to, elsewhere, far, farther on, here, in the back, in the distance, in the front, near, nearby, neighboring on, next to, on the other side, opposite to, overhead, there, to the left, to the right, to the side, under, underneath, wherever*
- **Purpose/cause and effect:** *accordingly, as a consequence, as a result, because, consequently, due to, for that reason, for this purpose, hence, in order that, on account of, since, so, so that, then, therefore, thereupon, thus, to do this, to this end, with this in mind, with this objective*
- **Qualification:** *almost, although, always, frequently, habitually, maybe, nearly, never, oftentimes, often, perhaps, probably, time and again*
- **Result:** *accordingly, and so, as a result, as an outcome, consequently, hence, so, then, therefore, thereupon, thus*
- **Similarity:** *again, also, and, as well as, besides, by the same token, for example, furthermore, in a like manner, in a similar way, in the same way, like, likewise, moreover, once more, similarly, so*
- **Summary or conclusion:** *after all, all in all, as a result, as has been noted, as I have said, as we have seen, as mentioned earlier, as stated, clearly, finally, in any event, in brief, in conclusion, in other words, in particular, in short, in simpler terms, in summary, on the whole, that is, therefore, to conclude, to summarize*
- **Time:** *after a bit, after a few days, after a while, afterward, again, also, and then, as long as, as soon as, at first, at last, at length, at that time, at the same time, before, during, earlier, eventually, finally, first, following, formerly, further, hence, initially, immediately, in a few days, in the first place, in the future, in the meantime, in the past, last, lately, later, meanwhile, next, now, on (a certain day), once, previously, recently, second, shortly, simultaneously, since, so far, soon, still, then, thereafter, this time, today, tomorrow, until, until now, when, whenever*

Right: *I liked Angela so I asked her on a date; unfortunately, it didn't work out.*

Wrong: *The Achilles' heel of Roger was his inability to make head nor tails of romantic relationships.*

Clichés and Redundancies

Do any of the phrases in the previous sentence sound familiar? Have you heard them used dozens, if not hundreds, of times? Do they sound stale and meaningless? Yes? That's because they're clichés.

Clichés and redundancies can really clutter your writing. They can distract and annoy your readers and, perhaps worst of all, they can completely obscure your message. You can more easily avoid them by becoming aware of their use in everyday life.

A cliché is a worn-out expression, one you've heard over and over, or time and time again, or a thousand times before (do you get the picture?). It may have been clever or had a special meaning the first time you heard it, but by now you've come across it so many times that it's lost its pizzazz and so doesn't add any spice to your writing.

As a rule, you should avoid using clichés because they're unoriginal, stale, and monotonous. Your readers won't think your work is the least bit creative if all they see is cliché-ridden writing.

Most likely, you're familiar with hundreds of clichés. If you read the first part of a phrase and you can fill in its ending, then your phrase is probably a cliché.

Take a look at the first parts of these phrases:

put all your eggs	_____
there's more there than meets	_____
read the handwriting	_____
costs an arm	_____
every cloud has	_____
that's the way the	_____

You know the ending for each of those, don't you? That's how you know they're clichés. Just in case you're don't, though, here are the endings:

put all your eggs in one basket
there's more there than meets the eye
read the handwriting on the wall
costs an arm and a leg
every cloud has a silver lining
that's the way the cookie crumbles

Good Grammar Tip

Many clichés are also similes (comparisons using *like* or *as*). You're probably familiar with the following expressions:

happy as a lark	slippery as an eel
pretty as a picture	fit as a fiddle
blind as a bat	snug as a bug in a rug
dumb as a post	high as a kite
sharp as a tack	

One way to tell if the image you're using is clichéd is to call to your mind a visual image of the phrase. When you hear *Achilles' heel*, what comes to mind? Do you know the origin of the phrase? Do you know that when the Greek hero Achilles was a baby, his mother dipped him in the River Styx to make him invulnerable—but since she held him by his heel, that was his only weak spot? If you think your readers won't know this, it's time to look for a better, more evocative image. (In fact, sometimes, even if the reader *does* know the myth, it's still a cliché.)

When you're getting ideas or writing your first draft, sometimes you'll think of a cliché. Go ahead and write it down. But when you revise your work, get out your eraser (or press the Delete key) pronto and get rid of that cliché.

If you can't think of an original way to reword your cliché, try "translating" it in a literal way. Say, for instance, that you've written:

• *It was plain as the nose on his face that Corey wouldn't stick his neck out for anybody else.*

In that sentence, you're dealing with two clichés (*plain as the nose on his face* and *stick his neck out*). To make the sentence cliché-free, you could change it to:

- *Plainly, Corey wouldn't take a risk for anybody else.*

Is there any time that using a cliché is permissible? Sure. The style for using an occasional cliché is relaxed or casual, so keep in mind that clichés have no place in academic writing. But if your style allows you to use a cliché in a humorous way, go ahead and add one occasionally. For instance, you might be writing about nobility in Europe. With a casual tone, you might use this expanded cliché as your title: "Putting Up Your Dukes (and Earls)."

Good Grammar Tip

It is permissible to use clichés in academic writing if you are quoting someone. You must quote the dialogue exactly in such a case.

The trick is to let your reader know that you're using a cliché intentionally. If you're in a pinch (yes, that's a cliché), write something along the lines of *Even though I knew the cliché 'Little pitchers have big ears,'* and then go on to elaborate on how the cliché fits in with your topic.

Now let's move on to the common and annoying habit of many writers redundancies:

- *I've said it before and I'll say it again.*

- *I've said it before, but now I'll reiterate.*

- *I've said it before and I'd like to repeat myself.*

We've all heard words like these before—and, odds are, hearing people repeat themselves drives most of us crazy. When it comes to writing, using redundant words or phrases not only diminishes the value of your work, it's also a waste of your readers' time.

Take a look at the following commonly seen or often heard redundant phrases and read the explanations about why they're redundant. (Get ready to smack yourself on the head as you mutter, "I should have thought of that"—but comfort yourself with the thought that you're certainly not alone in using these phrases!) Then start cutting your own redundancies.

Redundant Phrase	Explanation
advance planning	Planning must be done in advance. Delete *advance*.
A.M. in the morning	*A.M.* means *morning*. Delete *in the morning*.
and also	Use one word or the other, but not both.
as an added bonus	If something is a bonus, it must be added. Delete *added*.
ask the question	You can't ask anything except a question; delete *the question*.
ATM machine	The *M* in *ATM* stands for *machine*. Delete *machine*.
basic essentials	If they're the essentials, they have to be basic. Delete *basic*.
cash money	Is cash ever anything but money? Delete *cash*.
close proximity	You can't have far proximity, can you? Delete *close*.
closed fist	A fist must be closed. Delete *closed*.
combined together	Things that are combined must be together. Delete *together*.
completely unanimous	Something cannot be partially unanimous. Delete *completely*.
continue on	Can you continue off? Delete *on*.
cooperate together	You can't cooperate apart. Delete *together*.
each and every	The words mean the same thing; delete one.

Redundant Phrase	Explanation
end result	Can you have a result that's not in the end? Delete *end*.
estimated at about	*Estimated* means *about*. Delete *at about*.
exactly the same	If something is the same, it must be exact. Delete *the same*.
excised out	You can't excise in, can you? Delete *out*.
foreign imports	Material that's imported must be foreign. Delete *foreign*.
free gift (free gratis)	If it's a gift or is gratis, it's free. Delete *free*.
HIV virus	The *V* in *HIV* stands for *virus*. Delete *virus*.
honest truth	If something isn't the truth, it isn't honest. Delete *honest*.
important essentials	If items are essential, surely they're important. Delete *important*.
large in size	The word *large* denotes size. Delete *in size*.
mutual cooperation	Cooperation has to be mutual. Delete *mutual*.
my own personal opinion	*My opinion* means it's your own and it's personal. Delete *own personal*.
overused cliché	If a phrase isn't overused, it's not a cliché. Delete *overused*.
past memory	You can't have a future memory, can you? Delete *past*.
PIN number	The *N* in *PIN* stands for *number*. Delete *number*.
P.M. at night	P.M. means night. Delete *at night*.
return back	Here again, it's hard to return forward. Delete *back*.

Redundant Phrase	Explanation
roast beef with au jus	The *au* means *with*; delete *with*.
safe haven	By definition, a haven is a safe place. Delete *safe*.
sudden impulse	An impulse is sudden, or it's not an impulse. Delete *sudden*.
sum total	If you have a sum, you have a total. Delete one word or the other.
totally monopolize	A monopoly is total, isn't it? Delete *totally*.
true fact	By definition, a fact must be true. Delete *true*.
valuable asset	If something is an asset, then it has value. Delete *valuable*.

Right: *Roger's weakness was his inability to figure out romantic relationships.*

Appendix A

Some Grammar Resources

If you want further assistance with punctuation, spelling, or usage, there is a vast body of resources available to help you. Here are some of them to get you started.

Books

Hacker, Diana, and Nancy Sommers, *A Writer's Reference.* Bedford/St. Martins, 2010.

Lester, Mark, and Larry Beason, *McGraw-Hill Handbook of English Grammar and Usage, Second Edition: With 160 Exercises.* McGraw-Hill, 2012.

O'Conner, Patricia T., *Woe Is I: The Grammarphobe's Guide to Better English in Plain English, Third Edition.* Riverhead, 2010.

Strunk, William Jr., and E.B. White, *The Elements of Style, Fourth Edition.* Longman, 1999.

Thurman, Susan, *The Only Grammar Book You'll Ever Need,* Adams Media, 2003.

Truss, Lynne, *Eats, Shoots & Leaves: The Zero Tolerance Approach to Punctuation,* Gotham, 2006.

Turabian, Kate L., *A Manual for Writers of Research Papers, Theses, and Dissertations, Eighth Edition.* University of Chicago Press, 2013.

Zinsser, William, *On Writing Well: The Classic Guide to Writing Nonfiction, 30th Anniversary Edition.* Harper Perennial, 2006.

Online
Blue Falcon Editing

More than 150 language tips (and growing), along with tips on writing fiction and nonfiction.

www.bluefalconediting.com/resources

Common Errors in English Usage
Run by Paul Brians, Emeritus Professor of English, Washington State University. It's a good guide to usage.
www.wsu.edu/~brians/errors.com

GrammarBook.com
Started by the late Jane Straus, the author of *The Blue Book of Grammar and Punctuation*, includes lists of rules and sample quizzes to test your knowledge.
www.grammarbook.com

Grammar Bytes!
This site provides quizzes, handouts, and tips.
www.chompchomp.com/menu.htm

Grammar Girl
Answers grammar questions in a concise, easy-to-understand manner, often using examples.
www.quickanddirtytips.com/grammar-girl

Guide to Grammar & Writing
Includes grammar tips, a guide to writing research papers, quizzes, and more.
http://grammar.ccc.commnet.edu/grammar/

Appendix B

COMMON IRREGULAR VERBS

The good news is that most English verbs form their past and past participle by adding -d or -ed to the base form of the verb (the form you'd find listed first in the dictionary). These are called regular verbs.

The bad news is that English has a number of verb forms that aren't formed in that way; some people call them "those %*#@^ verbs," but usually they're called irregular verbs (clever, huh?).

Just to keep you on your toes, two verbs—*hang* and *lie*—may be regular or irregular, depending on their meaning in the sentence. If *hang* means *to use a noose*, it's a regular verb. If it means *to affix to a wall*, it's irregular. For example:

• *Prison officials discovered a picture the hanged man's mother had hung in his cell.*

If *lie* means *to tell a falsehood*, it's a regular verb. If it means *to rest or recline*, it's irregular. Here's an example:

• *Dave lay on the beach and lied when he phoned in sick.*

Here's a list of often-used irregular English verbs:

Base (Infinitive)	Simple Past	Past Participle
abide	abode/abided	abode/abided
arise	arose	arisen
awake	awoke/awaked	awaked/awoken
be	was, were	been
bear	bore	borne/born
beat	beat	beaten/beat
become	became	become
befall	befell	befallen

begin	began	begun
behold	beheld	beheld
bend	bent	bent
beseech	besought/beseeched	besought/beseeched
beset	beset	beset
bet	bet/betted	bet/betted
bid	bade/bid	bidden/bid
bind	bound	bound
bite	bit	bitten/bit
bleed	bled	bled
blow	blew	blown
break	broke	broken
breed	bred	bred
bring	brought	brought
broadcast	broadcast/broadcasted	broadcast/broadcasted
browbeat	browbeat	browbeaten
build	built	built
burn	burned/burnt	burned/burnt
burst	burst	burst
bust	busted	busted
buy	bought	bought
cast	cast	cast
catch	caught	caught
choose	chose	chosen
cling	clung	clung
come	came	come
cost	cost	cost
creep	crept	crept
cut	cut	cut
deal	dealt	dealt
dig	dug	dug

dive	dived/dove	dived
do	did	done
draw	drew	drawn
dream	dreamed/dreamt	dreamed/dreamt
drink	drank	drunk
drive	drove	driven
dwell	dwelt/dwelled	dwelt/dwelled
eat	ate	eaten
fall	fell	fallen
feed	fed	fed
feel	felt	felt
fight	fought	fought
find	found	found
fit	fitted/fit	fit
flee	fled	fled
fling	flung	flung
fly	flew	flown
forsake	forsook	forsaken
freeze	froze	frozen
get	got	gotten/got
gild	gilded/gilt	gilded/gilt
give	gave	given
go	went	gone
grind	ground	ground
grow	grew	grown
hang (to suspend)	hung	hung
has	had	had
have	had	had
hear	heard	heard
hew	hewed	hewn/hewed
hide	hid	hidden/hid

hit	hit	hit
hold	held	held
hurt	hurt	hurt
input	input	input
inset	inset	inset
interbreed	interbred	interbred
keep	kept	kept
kneel	knelt/kneeled	knelt/kneeled
knit	knit/knitted	knit/knitted
know	knew	known
lay	laid	laid
lead	led	led
lean	leaned	leaned
leap	leaped/leapt	leaped/leapt
learn	learned/learnt	learned/learnt
leave	left	left
lend	lent	lent
lie (to rest or recline)	lay	lain
light	lighted/lit	lighted/lit
lose	lost	lost
make	made	made
mean	meant	meant
meet	met	met
mistake	mistook	mistaken
mow	mowed	mowed/mown
outbid	outbid	outbid
outdo	outdid	outdone
outgrow	outgrew	outgrown
outrun	outran	outrun
outsell	outsold	outsold
partake	partook	partaken

pay	paid	paid
plead	pleaded/pled	pleaded/pled
proofread	proofread	proofread
prove	proved/proven	proved/proven
put	put	put
quit	quit/quitted	quit/quitted
read	read	read
rid	rid/ridded	rid/ridded
ride	rode	ridden
ring	rang	rung
rise	rose	risen
run	ran	run
saw (to cut)	sawed	sawed/sawn
say	said	said
see	saw	seen
seek	sought	sought
sell	sold	sold
send	sent	sent
set	set	set
sew	sewed	sewn/sewed
shake	shook	shaken
shave	shaved	shaved/shaven
shear	sheared	sheared/shorn
shed	shed	shed
shine	shone/shined	shone/shined
shoe	shod	shod/shodden
shoot	shot	shot
show	showed	shown/showed
shrink	shrank/shrunk	shrunk/shrunken
shut	shut	shut
sing	sang/sung	sung

sink	sank/sunk	sunk
sit	sat	sat
slay	slew	slain
sleep	slept	slept
slide	slid	slid
sling	slung	slung
slit	slit	slit
smell	smelled/smelt	smelled/smelt
smite	smote	smitten/smote
sow	sowed	sown/sowed
speak	spoke	spoken
speed	sped/speeded	sped/speeded
spell	spelled/spelt	spelled/spelt
spend	spent	spent
spill	spilled/spilt	spilled/spilt
spin	spun	spun
spit	spat/spit	spat/spit
split	split	split
spoil	spoiled/spoilt	spoiled/spoilt
spoon-feed	spoon-fed	spoon-fed
spread	spread	spread
spring	sprang/sprung	sprung
stand	stood	stood
steal	stole	stolen
stick	stuck	stuck
sting	stung	stung
stink	stank/stunk	stunk
strew	strewed	strewn/strewed
stride	strode	stridden
strike	struck	struck/stricken
string	strung	strung

strive	strove	striven/strived
swear	swore	sworn
sweep	swept	swept
swell	swelled	swelled/swollen
swim	swam	swum
swing	swung	swung
take	took	taken
teach	taught	taught
tear	tore	torn
tell	told	told
think	thought	thought
thrive	thrived/throve	thrived/thriven
throw	threw	thrown
tread	trod	trodden/trod
understand	understood	understood
uphold	upheld	upheld
upset	upset	upset
wake	woke/waked	waked/woken
wear	wore	worn
weave	wove	woven
wed	wedded	wed/wedded
weep	wept	wept
wet	wet/wetted	wet/wetted
win	won	won
wind	wound	wound
wring	wrung	wrung

Appendix C

COMMONLY MISUSED WORDS AND PHRASES

Need a little advice (or should that be advise*?) about when to use certain words? Are you feeling alright (or* all right*?) about your ability to distinguish between (or is that* among*?)* alumni, alumnae, alumnus, *and* alumna*? Could you use an angel (or an* angle*?) on your shoulder to give you some guidance? Are you anxious—or are you* eager*?—to overcome your brain freeze about when to use particular words?*

Not to worry! This appendix contains an extensive list of words that are commonly misused or confused. Also included are a number of mnemonics to help you remember the differences when this book isn't handy (although you *should* carry it with you at all times!).

Here are the words that cause some of the greatest perplexity and befuddlement:

a, an: Use *a* before words that begin with a consonant sound (*a* pig; *a* computer); use *an* before words that begin with a vowel sound (*an* earring, *an* integer). The sound is what makes the difference. Write *a habit* because *habit* starts with the *h* sound after the article, but write *an honor* because the *h* in *honor* isn't pronounced (the first sound of *honor* is the vowel *o*).

• *What an honor and a privilege it's to meet a history expert like Prof. Maltby.*

a lot, alot, allot: Okay, let's begin with the fact that there is no such word as *alot*. If you mean a great number of people or things, use *a lot.*

Here's a mnemonic for this: *a whole lot* is two whole words. If you mean *allocate*, use *allot.* A mnemonic for *allot* is *all*ocate = *all*ot.

• *Tomorrow night, the mayor will allot a lot of money for various municipal projects.*

accept, except: *Accept* has several meanings, including *believe, take on, endure,* and *consent; except* means *excluding.* If your sentence can keep its meaning if you substitute *excluding,* use *except.*

• *Except for food for the volunteers, Doris wouldn't accept any donations.*

adapt, adopt: To ad*a*pt is to ch*a*nge; to ad*o*pt is to take and make your *o*wn.
• *After Mary Elizabeth and Ron adopted the baby, they learned to adapt to having little sleep.*

advice, advise: *Advise* is what you do when you give *advice*. Here's a mnemonic to help you remember: To adv*ise* you must be w*ise*. Good adv*ice* is to drive slowly on *ice*.
• *Grandpa tried to advise me when I was a youngster, but I wouldn't listen to his advice.*

affect, effect: *Affect* is usually a verb (something that shows action), usually means *change* or *shape*, and—as a verb—has its accent on the first syllable. (There is a meaning of *affect* as a noun, but unless you're a psychologist you needn't worry about it.) *Effect* is almost always a noun meaning *result* or *outcome*, *appearance* or *impression* (*effect* has a rare use as a verb, when it means *to achieve* or *cause*). One mnemonic to help you remember is this: Caus*e* and *e*ffect (that is, if you want the word that is used in this phrase, you want *effect*—the word that begins with the last letter of *cause*).
• *The effect of the announcement of impending war won't affect Adam's decision to join the military.*

aggravate, annoy: If you mean *pester* or *irritate*, you want *annoy*. Aggravate means *exaggerate* or *make worse*.
• *Steven was annoyed when his boss aggravated the situation by talking to the press.*

aid, aide: If you help, you *aid*; if you have a help*er* or support*er*, you have an aid*e*.
• *The aid from my aide is invaluable.*

aisle, isle, I'll: An *aisle* is in a theater; an *isle* is an island (a shortened form of the word); *I'll* is short for *I will*.
• *I'll walk down the aisle to meet my groom; then we'll honeymoon on a desert isle.*

all ready, already: If you mean all is ready, use *all ready*; if you mean in the past, use *already*.
• *I already told you we're all ready to go out to dinner!*

all right, alright: *All right* is always two words, although you often see the incorrect spelling *alright*. You wouldn't say something is *aleft* or *alwrong*, would you? (Please say you wouldn't!)
• *Is it all right if we eat in tonight?*

all together, altogether: *All together* means *simultaneously* or *all at once*; *altogether* means *entirely* or *wholly*. If you can substitute *entirely* or *wholly* in the sentence and the meaning doesn't change, you need the form of the word that is entirely, wholly one word.

• *You're altogether wrong about the six friends going all together to the dance; each is going separately.*

alumni, alumnae, alumnus, alumna: You can thank the Romans for this confusion; Latin had separate words for masculine, feminine, singular, and plural forms. Here's the rundown: One male graduate is an *alumnus*; one female graduate is an *alumna*; several female graduates are *alumnae*; and several male graduates or several male and female graduates are *alumni*. You can see why the short form *alum* is often used informally; when you use it, you don't have to look up the right form of the word.

• *Although Mary Jo and her sisters are alumnae from Wellesley, Mary Jo is the alumna who receives the most attention; her brothers Martin and Xavier are alumni of Harvard, but Martin is a more famous alumnus than Xavier.*

allusion, illusion: An *allusion* is a reference; an *illusion* is a false impression. If you want a word that means mistaken idea, you want *illusion*.

• *Kay told Jerry that she was under the illusion he'd be her Prince Charming; Jerry didn't understand the allusion.*

altar, alter: If you change something, you *alter* it; you worship before an *altar*.

• *We'll alter the position of the altar so the congregation can see the new carvings.*

among, between: Think division. If only two people are dividing something, use *between*; if more than two people are involved, use *among*. Here's a mnemonic: be*tw*een for *tw*o and among for a *g*roup.

• *The money was divided between Sarah and Bob; the land was divided among Billy, Henry, and Lillian.*

angel, angle: An *angel* has wings; the degree of an angle is often studied.

• *The angel's wings are set at ninety-degree angles from its body.*

anxious, eager: These two words are often confused. If you're *anxious*, you're nervous or concerned; if you're *eager*, you're enthusiastic.

• *I had been anxious about my medical test results, but when they proved negative I was eager to kick up my heels.*

anybody, any body: *Anybody* means *any one person* (and is usually interchangeable with *anyone*). *Any body* refers (pardon the graphic reference) to one dead person.

• *Anybody can help search for any body that might not have been found in the wreckage.*

appraise, apprise: To ap*praise* is to give value to something (to see how much *praise* it needs); to appr*ise* is to *i*nform.
• *The auctioneer called to apprise our family about how he would appraise various items for us.*

bad, badly: When you're writing about how you feel, use *bad*. However, if you're writing about how you did something or performed or reacted to something, use *badly* (twisted your ankle *badly*; played *badly* in the game).
• *Gregg felt bad he had scored so badly on the test.*

bazaar, bizarre: The first is a marketplace; the second means *strange, weird,* or *peculiar.*
• *The most bizarre purchase that came from the bazaar was a pair of sandals without any soles.*

bear, bare: A b*ear* can t*ear* off your *ear*; if you're bar*e*, you're nud*e*.
• *The bare bathers were disturbed when the grizzly bear arrived.*

besides, beside: If you want the one that means *in addition to*, you want the one that has an additional *s* (*besides*); *beside* means *by the side of.*

• *Besides her groom, the bride wanted her dad beside her in the photo.*

breath, breathe: You take a *breath*; you inhal*e* and *e*xhal*e* when you breath*e*.
• *In the cold of the winter, it was hard for me to breathe when taking a breath outside.*

cavalry, Calvary: The *cavalry* are soldiers on horseback (the word isn't capitalized unless it begins a sentence); Ca*l*vary is the hi*l*l where Christ was crucified (and is always capitalized).
• *The cavalry wasn't in attendance for the march up Calvary.*

can, may: If you *can* do something, you're physically able to do it. If you *may* do it, you have permission to do it.
• *You can use "ain't" in a sentence, but you may not.*

cannot, am not, is not, are not, and all other "nots": For some strange reason, *cannot* is written as one word. All other words that have *not* with them are written as two words. Go figure.

capital, capitol: The *capitol* is the building in which the legislative body meets. If you mean the one in Washington, D.C., use a capital *C*; if you mean the one in your state, use a lowercase *c*. Remember that the building (the one spelled with an *o*) usually has a dome. Use *capital* with all other meanings.

• *The capital spent by the legislators at the capitol is appalling.*

carat, caret, carrot, karat: A *carat* is a weight for a stone (a diamond, for instance); *carat* is also an alternate spelling of *karat*, which is a measurement of how much gold is in an alloy (as in the abbreviation 18k; the *k* is for *karat*). A *caret* is this proofreading mark: ^ (meaning that you should insert something at that point). Finally, a *carrot* is the orange vegetable your mother told you to eat.

• *Set in an eighteen-karat gold band, the five-carat diamond was shaped like a carrot.*

censor, censure: To censor is to take out the bad material; to *censure* is to place blame (don't cen*sure* someone unless you're *sure*).

• *The full Senate voted not to censure the senator for trying to censor the e-mail that came to other congressional employees.*

cite, sight, site: Your *sight* is your vision or a view (you use your *sight* to look at a beautiful *sight*); to *cite* is to make reference to a specific source; a *site* is a location, such as on the Internet.

• *The colors on the website you cited in your paper were a sight to behold.*

climactic, climatic: *Climactic* refers to a climax, a pinnacle; *climatic* is related to the weather (the climate).

• *Last year's weather featured many climatic oddities, but the climactic point came when snow arrived in June.*

coarse, course: If something is *coarse*, it's rough; *oars* are c*oarse*. A c*ourse* is a r*oute*, a class, or part of the idiomatic phrase *of course*.

• *The racecourse led the runners over coarse terrain.*

complement, compliment: If something completes another thing, it *complements* it (comple*te* = comple*ment*). If you receive praise, you've gotten a *compliment* (*I* like to receive a compl*i*ment).

• *The jewelry will complement the outfit the star will wear, and she will surely receive many compliments on her attire.*

conscience, conscious: Your *conscience* tells you whether something is right or wrong; if you're *conscious*, you're awake and aware.

• *On the witness stand, Marie said she wasn't conscious of the fact that her conscience told her not to steal the ashtray from the hotel room.*

continual, continuous: *Continuous* actions go on uninterrupted; *continual* actions are intermittent.

• *The continual rains lasted for ten days; because of that, the Blacksons had a continuous problem with water in their basement.*

core, corps, corpse: A *core* is a center or main section; a *corps* is a group or organization; a *corpse* is a dead body.
• *At the core of the Marine Corps lieutenant's sleeplessness was his discovery of a corpse while on a training mission.*

council, counsel: A *council* is an official group, a committee; to *counsel* is to give advice (the stock broker coun*sel*ed me to *sel*l).
• *The town council decided to counsel the youth group on the proper way to ask for funds.*

desert, dessert: A *desert* is a dry, arid place or (usually used in the plural form) a deserved reward or punishment (*just deserts*). The verb that means *to leave* is also *desert*. The food that is *s*o *s*weet is a de*ss*ert.
• *While lost in the desert, Rex craved a dessert of apple pie à la mode.*

device, devise: A *device* is a machine or tool; to *devise* means *to invent* or *concoct something.*
• *To devise, you must be wise. Will this device work on ice?*

discreet, discrete: *Discreet* means *cautious, careful,* or *guarded in conduct* (be discreet about whom you m*ee*t). *Discrete* means *separate* or *disconnected.*
• *The dancer's discreet movements were discrete from those performed by the rest of the chorus.*

dual, duel: The first means *two* (*dual* purposes); the second is a fight or contest (the lover's jealousy was f*uel* for the d*uel*).
• *The dual reasons for the duel were revenge and money.*

elicit, illicit: To *e*licit something is to *e*xtract it, to bring it out; something *ill*icit is *ill*egal.
• *The telephone scam artist engaged in the illicit practice of trying to elicit credit card information.*

emigrate, immigrate: To *e*migrate is to *e*xit a country; to *i*mmigrate is to come *i*nto a country.
• *Ten people were trying to emigrate from the tyranny of their country and immigrate to the United States.*

eminent, imminent: Someone well known is *e*minent; something that might take place *imm*ediately is *imm*inent.
• *Our meeting with the eminent scientist is imminent.*

ensure, insure: To *ensure* is to *make certain of something; insure* is only for business purposes (to *insure* a car).

• *To ensure that we continue to insure your house, send payment immediately.*

everyday, every day: *Everyday* means *routine* or *daily* (*everyday* low cost); *every day* means *every single day* (low prices *every day*). Use *single* words if you mean every *single* day.
• *The everyday inexpensive prices of the store meant that more shoppers came every day.*

faze, phase: To *faze* is to *intimidate* or *disturb*. As a noun, a *phase* is *a period of time*; as a verb, it means *to establish gradually*.
• *I wasn't fazed by his wish to phase out our relationship.*

fewer, less: Use *fewer* to describe plural words; use *less* to describe singular words.
• *The new product has fewer calories but less fat.*

figuratively, literally: *Literally* means *precisely as described*; *figuratively* means *in a symbolic or metaphoric way*.
• *When Pauline called, she asked if I was off my rocker; I thought she meant figuratively and wondered why she thought I had gone crazy. However, she intended to be taken literally, as she wondered if I was still sitting outside in my rocker.*

flaunt, flout: If you *flaunt* something, you show it off (*flaunt* your new jewelry); to *flout* is to jeer at someone or something in a contemptible way, or to intentionally disobey (*flout* the laws).
• *In an attempt to flaunt his new car to the girls on the other side of the road, James decided to flout the law and not stop at the red light.*

forego, forgo: If you mean something that has gone be*fore*, use *fore*go (a *foregone* conclusion); if you want the word that means *to do without something*, use *forgo* (the one that is without the *e*).
• *It's a foregone conclusion that Meg and Marion will forgo sweets when they're dieting.*

foreword, forward: The word that means *the opening information in a book* is *foreword* (it comes be*fore* the first important *word* of the book); for any other meaning, use *forward*.
• *To gain insight into the author's intent, you should read the foreword before you move forward in the book.*

foul, fowl: The animal is a *fowl*; the action on the basketball court is a *foul*; a bad odor smells *foul*.
• *The foul smell came from the fowl that had been slaughtered.*

good, well: *Good* is an adjective; it doesn't mean in *a high-quality manner,* or *correctly.* If you want either of those meanings you need an adverb, so you want *well.*

• *You did well on the test; your grade should be good.*

graduated, graduated from: A school *graduates* you; you *graduate from* a school.

• *The year Tiya Hudson graduated from college, the school graduated 5,000 students.*

grisly, grizzly: A horrible or gruesome sight is *grisly;* the North American bear is a *grizzly.*

• *A grisly scene was left after the attack by the grizzly bear.*

hanged, hung: People are *hanged* (did they *hang* the entire *gang* of desperadoes?); artwork is *hung.*

• *The gruesome picture of the hanged man was hung on the wall.*

heal, heel: To *heal* means to *cure* or *patch up* (to *heal* a wound); among other verb definitions, *to heel* is *to tilt to one side, to give money to,* or *to urge along;* a *well-heeled* person has a *considerable amount of money.*

• *You might need ointment to heal the blisters you get from trying to right the sails when the ship heels in the wind.*

hear, here: You h*ear* with your *ear. Here* is the opposite of t*here.*

• *Did you hear that Aunt Helen is here?*

hopefully: If you mean *I hope,* or *it's hoped,* then that's what you should write. *Hopefully* means *confidently* or *with anticipation.*

• *The director waited hopefully for the Oscar nominations to be announced.*

imply, infer: Both of these have to do with words not said aloud. A speaker im*p*lies something; a liste*n*er i*n*fers something.

• *Rufus thought the boss had implied that she would be back for an inspection next week, but Ruth didn't infer that.*

in, into: *In* means with*in; into* means from the outside *to* the *in*side.

• *Go into the house, look in my purse, and bring me money.*

its, it's: *It's* means only *it is* (before *it's* too late); *its* means *belonging to it* (I gave the dog *its* food and water).

• *It's a shame the dog lost its bone.*

lay, lie: Now I *lay* my head on the pillow; last night I *laid* my head on the pillow; in the past I have *laid* my head on the pillow. If it helps to remember the difference, the forms of *lay* (meaning *to put or place*) are transitive (they take an object). Today I *lie* in the sun; yesterday I *lay* in the sun; in the past I have *lain* in the sun. The forms of *lie* (meaning *to rest or recline*) are intransitive (they take no object).

• *As I lay in bed, I wondered where I had laid my watch.*

lead, led: If you want the word that means *was in charge of* or *guided*, use *led*; otherwise, use *lead*.

• *The company, led by one of the richest people in the world, announced that its CEO was retiring; today a newcomer will lead it.*

loose, lose: *Loose* (which rhymes with *noose*) means *not tight*. *Lose* is the opposite of *find* or *win*.

• *Will I lose my belt if it's too loose?*

may of, might of, must of, should of, would of, could of: In speech, we slur these phrases so that they all sound as if they end in *of*, but in fact all of them end in *have*. Their correct forms are *may have, might have, must have, should have, would have,* and *could have.*

• *I must have thought you would have been able to find the room without directions.*

moral, morale: If something is *moral*, it's *right* or *ethical* (that's the adjective form); if something has a *moral*, it has a *message* or a *meaning* (that's the noun form). Your moral*e* is your *e*steem.

• *The moral high road that the politician took boosted the morale of the entire staff.*

myself, itself, yourself, himself, herself, themselves, ourselves, yourselves: None of these pronouns should ever be used without the antecedent that corresponds to it.

• *You might write: I myself would like to go for a drive. But you shouldn't write, "Mike took Pat and myself for a drive."*

nauseated, nauseous: *Nauseous* is often misused; it means *disgusting* or *sickening*; *nauseated* means *sick to your stomach* (you can get nause*ated* from something you *ate*).

• *The nauseous fumes caused the workers to become nauseated.*

pacific, specific: *P*acific means *peaceful*; *specific* means *precise* or *individualized*.

• *To be specific, the pacific view from Hickory Mountain is what calms me the most.*

passed, past: *Passed* is a verb; *past* is an adjective (p*ast* often means l*ast*) or noun meaning *the preceding time*.

• *In the past, twenty parades have passed down this street.*

peace, piece: Pe*ace* is the opposite of w*ar*; a *piece* is a part or portion (a pi*ece* of pie).

• *The father bargained with his small children, "Give me an hour's peace, and I'll get you a piece of cake."*

persecute, prosecute: To *persecute* is to *oppress or bully*; to *prosecute* is to *bring legal action*.

• *We warned our neighbors that we would prosecute if they continued to persecute their dog.*

pore, pour: If you *read something carefully*, you *pore* over it. If you make a liquid go *out* of a container, you *pour* it.

• *After Harry accidentally poured ink on the new floor, he pored over several books to find out how to clean the stain.*

prophecy, prophesy: You have a forecast or a prediction if you have a prophe*cy*. *Prophesy* is pronounced with the last syllable sounding like *sigh*, and you might sigh when you *prophesy* something dismal.

• *Last week the audience heard the medium prophesy about forthcoming bad weather; the prophecy has yet to come true.*

principle, principal: *Principle* means *law* or *belief*. *Principal* means *major* or *head*; it also means *money that earns interest in a bank*. The princi*pal* is the head person in a school; he or she is your *pal* and makes princi*pal* decisions.

• *That is the most important principle our principal believes.*

quiet, quite: *Quiet* is *calm* or *silence*; *quite* means *to a certain extent*. Be sure to check the ending of the word you use; that's where mistakes are made. Think: I hope my pet is qui*et*.

• *Are you quite sure that you were quiet in the library?*

real, really: *Real* means *actual* or *true*; *really* means *in truth* or *in reality*. Except in the most casual tone in writing, neither *real* nor *really* should be used in the sense of *very* (that's a *real* good song on the radio; I'm *really* glad you listened to that station).

• *When Debbie and Phillip realized they were lost, the real importance of carrying a compass hit them.*

respectfully, respectively: If you're *full* of respect for someone and want to show it, you do it respect*fully*. *Respectively* means *in the order stated*.

• *Upon hearing the news, I respectfully called Bob and Janie, respectively.*

role, roll: A *role* is a *position or part* (in a production); a *roll* is a *piece of bread* on the dinner table; to *roll* is to *rotate*.

• *The role of the acrobat will be played by someone who can perform a backward roll.*

set, sit: If you place something, you set it. If you're in an upright position (like in a chair), you sit. In addition, *set* is transitive (it must have an object); *sit* is intransitive (it doesn't have an object).
• *Please set the table before you sit down.*

slow, slowly: *Slow* is an adjective, not an adverb. If you're using the word after *go*, *drive*, *walk*, or any other verb, use *slowly*.
• *I slowly walked. I walked at a slow pace.*

stalactite, stalagmite: Stalactites grow from the ceiling down; stalagmites grow from the ground up.
• *On a recent spelunking trip, I worried about tripping over the stalagmites and bumping into the stalactites.*

stationery, stationary: If you mean something that lacks any motion, use *stationary*; if you mean something you write a letter on, use stationery.
• *The stationery had a picture of people riding stationary bicycles.*

supposed (to): Often the d is incorrectly omitted from *supposed to* (meaning *expected to* or *designed to*).
• *In this job, you're supposed to be able to write short, clear, and effective memos.*

than, then: If you mean *next* or *therefore* or *at that time*, you want *then*. If you want the word that shows a comparison, use *than*.

• *For a while, Mary ran more quickly than I; then she dropped her pace.*

that, which: For clauses that don't need commas (restrictive clauses), use *that*. For nonrestrictive clauses, which need commas, use *which*.
• *The local dog kennels, which are nearby, are the ones that have been featured in the news lately.*

there, their, they're: If you want the opposite of *here*, use t*here*; if you mean they a*re*, you want they*'re*; if you mean belonging to *them*, use *their*.
• *There are employees who think they're going to get their 10 percent raises tomorrow.*

throne, thrown: If you can sit on it, it's a *throne* (you can sit *on* a thro*ne*); if something has been tossed, it's been *thrown*.
• *When the king was deposed, his throne was thrown out the window.*

to, too, two: If you mean something *additional*, it's the one with the *additional o* (*too*); *two* is the *number after one*; *to* means *in the direction of something.*
• *Did our supervisor ask the two new employees to go to Detroit and Chicago, too?*

troop, troupe: Both are groups of people, but *troupe* refers to performers only.

• *The troupe of actors performed for the troop of Brownies.*

try and, try to: Almost always the mistake comes in writing *try and* when you need to use *try to.*
• *The lady said she would try to get the dress in my size; I hoped she would try and keep looking.*

use to, used to: *Use to* means *employ for the purposes of*; *used to* (often misspelled without the d*)* means *formerly* or *in the past.*
• *I used to like to listen to the excuses people would use to leave work early.*

weather, whether: If you mean conditions of the climate, use *weather.* (Can you stand to *eat* in the h*eat* of this bad we*ather*?) If you mean *which, whichever,* or *if it's true that,* use *whether.*
• *It's now mid-April, and the weather can't decide whether it's spring or winter.*

when, where: If you're writing a definition, don't use either of these words. For instance, don't write "A charley horse is when you get a cramp in your leg"; instead, write something like: "A charley horse is the result of a cramp in your leg."
• *A bank is a place in which you can make a deposit or withdrawal.*

who, which, that: Don't use *which* when you're writing about people. Some style guides have the same restriction for *that* and some don't, so be sure to check.
• *The inspector, who gives the orders that we must obey, said that the law, which had never been enforced, would result in higher costs.*

whose, who's: *Whose* means *belonging to whom*; *who's* is short for *who is* (the apostrophe means the *i* has been omitted).
• *After the sock hop, who's going to determine whose shoes these are?*

woman, women: One *man,* two *men.* One wo*man,* two wo*men.* It's that simple.
• *The local woman asked the two visiting women if they'd like a tour of the town.*

your, you're: If you mean *belonging to you,* use *your* (this is *our* car; that is *your* car); if you mean *you are,* use *you're* (remember that the apostrophe means the *a* has been omitted).
• *If you're in the sun in Florida, be sure to put sunscreen on your nose.*

Index